PENGUIN BOOKS
Selected Poems

Born in Bromsgrove, Worcestershire, in 1932, Geoffrey
Hill is the author of three books of criticism and ten
books of poetry, including *The Triumph of Love*, co-
winner of the Heinemann Award. His *Collected Poems*,
Canaan, *The Triumph of Love*, *Speech! Speech!*, *The
Orchards of Syon*, *Scenes from Comus* and *Without
Title* are all published by Penguin.

Geoffrey Hill currently lives and teaches in Massachu-
setts, where he is Professor of Literature and Religion
at Boston University. He is also Honorary Fellow of
Keble College, Oxford; Honorary Fellow of Emmanuel
College, Cambridge; Fellow of the Royal Society of
Literature; and since 1996 Fellow of the American
Academy of Arts and Sciences.

Books by Geoffrey Hill

Selected Poems

GEOFFREY HILL

PENGUIN BOOKS

PENGUIN BOOKS

Published by the Penguin Group
Penguin Books Ltd, 80 Strand, London WC2R ORL, England
Penguin Group (USA) Inc., 375 Hudson Street, New York, New York 10014, USA
Penguin Group (Canada), 90 Eglinton Avenue East, Suite 700, Toronto, Ontario, Canada M4P 3YZ
(a division of Pearson Penguin Canada Inc.)
Penguin Ireland, 25 St Stephen's Green, Dublin 2, Ireland (a division of Penguin Books Ltd)
Penguin Group (Australia), 250 Camberwell Road, Camberwell,
Victoria 3124, Australia (a division of Pearson Australia Group Pty Ltd)
Penguin Books India Pvt Ltd, 11 Community Centre,
Panchsheel Park, New Delhi – 110 017, India
Penguin Group (NZ), cnr Airborne and Rosedale Roads, Albany,
Auckland 1310, New Zealand (a division of Pearson New Zealand Ltd)
Penguin Books (South Africa) (Pty) Ltd, 24 Sturdee Avenue,
Rosebank, Johannesburg 2196, South Africa

Penguin Books Ltd, Registered Offices: 80 Strand, London WC2R ORL, England

www.penguin.com

First published 2006
5

Copyright © Geoffrey Hill, 2006
All rights reserved

The moral right of the author has been asserted

'La Bufera' by Eugenio Montale © Arnoldo Mondadori Editore, Milano

Set in 10.75/12.75 pt Monotype Sabon
Typeset by Rowland Phototypesetting Ltd, Bury St Edmunds, Suffolk
Printed in England by Clays Ltd, St Ives plc

ISBN-13: 978-0-141-02500-1

www.greenpenguin.co.uk

Penguin Books is committed to a sustainable
future for our business, our readers and our
planet. This book is made from paper certified
by the Forest Stewardship Council.

Contents

For the Unfallen

Genesis

I

Against the burly air I strode
Crying the miracles of God.

And first I brought the sea to bear
Upon the dead weight of the land;
And the waves flourished at my prayer,
The rivers spawned their sand.

And where the streams were salt and full
The tough pig-headed salmon strove,
Ramming the ebb, in the tide's pull,
To reach the steady hills above.

II

The second day I stood and saw
The osprey plunge with triggered claw,
Feathering blood along the shore,
To lay the living sinew bare.

And the third day I cried: 'Beware
The soft-voiced owl, the ferret's smile,
The hawk's deliberate stoop in air,
Cold eyes, and bodies hooped in steel,
Forever bent upon the kill.'

III

And I renounced, on the fourth day,
This fierce and unregenerate clay,

Building as a huge myth for man
The watery Leviathan,

And made the long-winged albatross
Scour the ashes of the sea
Where Capricorn and Zero cross,
A brooding immortality –
Such as the charmed phoenix has
In the unwithering tree.

IV

The phoenix burns as cold as frost;
And, like a legendary ghost,
The phantom-bird goes wild and lost,
Upon a pointless ocean tossed.

So, the fifth day, I turned again
To flesh and blood and the blood's pain.

V

On the sixth day, as I rode
In haste about the works of God,
With spurs I plucked the horse's blood.

By blood we live, the hot, the cold,
To ravage and redeem the world:
There is no bloodless myth will hold.

And by Christ's blood are men made free
Though in close shrouds their bodies lie
Under the rough pelt of the sea;

Though Earth has rolled beneath her weight
The bones that cannot bear the light.

God's Little Mountain

Below, the river scrambled like a goat
Dislodging stones. The mountain stamped its foot,
Shaking, as from a trance. And I was shut
With wads of sound into a sudden quiet.

I thought the thunder had unsettled heaven;
All was so still. And yet the sky was cloven
By flame that left the air cold and engraven.
I waited for the word that was not given,

Pent up into a region of pure force,
Made subject to the pressure of the stars;
I saw the angels lifted like pale straws;
I could not stand before those winnowing eyes

And fell, until I found the world again.
Now I lack grace to tell what I have seen;
For though the head frames words the tongue has none.
And who will prove the surgeon to this stone?

Holy Thursday

Naked, he climbed to the wolf's lair;
He beheld Eden without fear,
Finding no ambush offered there
But sleep under the harbouring fur.

He said: 'They are decoyed by love
Who, tarrying through the hollow grove,
Neglect the seasons' sad remove.
Child and nurse walk hand in glove

As unaware of Time's betrayal,
Weaving their innocence with guile.
But they must cleave the fire's peril
And suffer innocence to fall.

I have been touched with that fire,
And have fronted the she-wolf's lair.
Lo, she lies gentle and innocent of desire
Who was my constant myth and terror.'

Merlin

I will consider the outnumbering dead:
For they are the husks of what was rich seed.
Now, should they come together to be fed,
They would outstrip the locusts' covering tide.

Arthur, Elaine, Mordred; they are all gone
Among the raftered galleries of bone.
By the long barrows of Logres they are made one,
And over their city stands the pinnacled corn.

The Turtle Dove

Love that drained her drained him she'd loved, though each
For the other's sake forged passion upon speech,
Bore their close days through sufferance towards night
Where she at length grasped sleep and he lay quiet

As though needing no questions, now, to guess
What her secreting heart could not well hide.
Her caught face flinched in half-sleep at his side.
Yet she, by day, modelled her real distress,

Poised, turned her cheek to the attending world
Of children and intriguers and the old;
Conversed freely, exercised, was admired,
Being strong to dazzle. All this she endured

To affront him. He watched her rough grief work
Under the formed surface of habit. She spoke
Like one long undeceived but she was hurt.
She denied more love, yet her starved eyes caught

His, devouring, at times. Then, as one self-dared,
She went to him, plied there; like a furious dove
Bore down with visitations of such love
As his lithe, fathoming heart absorbed and buried.

Solomon's Mines

To Bonamy Dobrée

Anything to have done!
(The eagle flagged to the sun)
To have discovered and disclosed
The buried thrones, the means used;

Spadework and symbol, each deed
Resurrecting those best dead
Priests, soldiers and kings;
Blazed-out, stripped-out things;

Anything to get up and go
(Let the hewn gates clash to)
Without looking round
Out of that strong land.

The Distant Fury of Battle

Grass resurrects to mask, to strangle,
Words glossed on stone, lopped stone-angel;
But the dead maintain their ground –
That there's no getting round –

Who in places vitally rest,
Named, anonymous; who test
Alike the endurance of yews
Laurels, moonshine, stone, all tissues;

With whom, under licence and duress,
There are pacts made, if not peace.
Union with the stone-wearing dead
Claims the born leader, the prepared

Leader, the devourers and all lean men.
Some, finally, learn to begin.
Some keep to the arrangement of love
(Or similar trust) under whose auspices move

Most subjects, toward the profits of this
Combine of doves and witnesses.
Some, dug out of hot-beds, are brought bare,
Not past conceiving but past care.

Requiem for the Plantagenet Kings

For whom the possessed sea littered, on both shores,
Ruinous arms; being fired, and for good,
To sound the constitution of just wars,
Men, in their eloquent fashion, understood.

Relieved of soul, the dropping-back of dust,
Their usage, pride, admitted within doors;
At home, under caved chantries, set in trust,
With well-dressed alabaster and proved spurs
They lie; they lie; secure in the decay
Of blood, blood-marks, crowns hacked and coveted,
Before the scouring fires of trial-day
Alight on men; before sleeked groin, gored head,
Budge through the clay and gravel, and the sea
Across daubed rock evacuates its dead.

Two Formal Elegies

For the Jews in Europe

Knowing the dead, and how some are disposed:
Subdued under rubble, water, in sand graves,
In clenched cinders not yielding their abused
Bodies and bonds to those whom war's chance saves
Without the law: we grasp, roughly, the song.
Arrogant acceptance from which song derives
Is bedded with their blood, makes flourish young
Roots in ashes. The wilderness revives,

Deceives with sweetness harshness. Still beneath
Live skin stone breathes, about which fires but play,
Fierce heart that is the iced brain's to command
To judgment – studied reflex, contained breath –
Their best of worlds since, on the ordained day,
This world came spinning from Jehovah's hand.

2

For all that must be gone through, their long death
Documented and safe, we have enough
Witnesses (our world being witness-proof).
The sea flickers, roars, in its wide hearth.
Here, yearly, the pushing midlanders stand
To warm themselves; men, brawny with life,
Women who expect life. They relieve
Their thickening bodies, settle on scraped sand.

Is it good to remind them, on a brief screen,
Of what they have witnessed and not seen?
(Deaths of the city that persistently dies . . .?)
To put up stones ensures some sacrifice.
Sufficient men confer, carry their weight.
(At whose door does the sacrifice stand or start?)

Picture of a Nativity

Sea-preserved, heaped with sea-spoils,
Ribs, keels, coral sores,
Detached faces, ephemeral oils,
Discharged on the world's outer shores,

A dumb child-king
Arrives at his right place; rests,
Undisturbed, among slack serpents; beasts
With claws flesh-buttered. In the gathering

Of bestial and common hardship
Artistic men appear to worship
And fall down; to recognize
Familiar tokens; believe their own eyes.

Above the marvel, each rigid head,
Angels, their unnatural wings displayed,
Freeze into an attitude
Recalling the dead.

Canticle for Good Friday

The cross staggered him. At the cliff-top
Thomas, beneath its burden, stood
While the dulled wood
Spat on the stones each drop
Of deliberate blood.

A clamping, cold-figured day
Thomas (not transfigured) stamped, crouched,
Watched
Smelt vinegar and blood. He,
As yet unsearched, unscratched,

And suffered to remain
At such near distance
(A slight miracle might cleanse
His brain
Of all attachments, claw-roots of sense)

In unaccountable darkness moved away,
The strange flesh untouched, carrion-sustenance
Of staunchest love, choicest defiance,
Creation's issue congealing (and one woman's).

The Guardians

The young, having risen early, had gone,
Some with excursions beyond the bay-mouth,
Some toward lakes, a fragile reflected sun.
Thunder-heads drift, awkwardly, from the south;

The old watch them. They have watched the safe
Packed harbours topple under sudden gales,
Great tides irrupt, yachts burn at the wharf
That on clean seas pitched their effective sails.

There are silences. These, too, they endure:
Soft comings-on; soft after-shocks of calm.
Quietly they wade the disturbed shore;
Gather the dead as the first dead scrape home.

After Cumae

The sun again unearthed, colours come up fresh,
The perennials; and the laurels'
Washable leaves, that seem never to perish,
Obscure the mouthy cave, the dumb grottoes.

From the beginning, in the known world, slide
Drawn echoing hulls, axes grate, and waves
Deposit in their shallow margins varied
Fragments of marine decay and waftage;

And the sometimes-abandoned gods confuse
With immortal essences men's brief lives,
Frequenting the exposed and pious: those
Who stray, as designed, under applied perils,

Whose doom is easy, venturing so far
Without need, other than to freeze or burn;
Their wake, on spread-out oceans, a healed scar
Fingered, themselves the curios of voyage.

Little Apocalypse
Hölderlin: 1770–1843

Abrupt tempter; close enough to survive
The sun's primitive renewing fury;
Scorched vistas where crawl the injured and brave:
This man stands sealed against their injury:

Hermetic radiance of great suns kept in:
Man's common nature suddenly too rare:
See, for the brilliant coldness of his skin,
The god cast, perfected, among fire.

from *Of Commerce and Society*

They sat. They stood about.
They were estranged. The air,
As water curdles from clear,
Fleshed the silence. They sat.

They were appalled. The bells
In hollowed Europe spilt
To the gods of coin and salt.
The sea creaked with worked vessels.

Thriving against façades the ignorant sea
Souses our public baths, statues, waste ground:
Archaic earth-shaker, fresh enemy
('The tables of exchange being overturned');

Drowns Babel in upheaval and display;
Unswerving, as were the admired multitudes
Silenced from time to time under its sway.
By all means let us appease the terse gods.

In Piam Memoriam

1

Created purely from glass the saint stands,
Exposing his gifted quite empty hands
Like a conjurer about to begin,
A righteous man begging of righteous men.

2

In the sun lily-and-gold-coloured,
Filtering the cruder light, he has endured,
A feature for our regard; and will keep;
Of worldly purity the stained archetype.

3

The scummed pond twitches. The great holly-tree,
Emptied and shut, blows clear of wasting snow,
The common, puddled substance: beneath,
Like a revealed mineral, a new earth.

To the (Supposed) Patron

Prodigal of loves and barbecues,
Expert in the strangest faunas, at home
He considers the lilies, the rewards.
There is no substitute for a rich man.
At his first entering a new province
With new coin, music, the barest glancing
Of steel or gold suffices. There are many
Tremulous dreams secured under that head.
For his delight and his capacity
To absorb, freshly, the inside-succulence
Of untoughened sacrifice, his bronze agents
Speculate among convertible stones
And drink desert sand. That no mirage
Irritate his mild gaze, the lewd noonday
Is housed in cool places, and fountains
Salt the sparse haze. His flesh is made clean.
For the unfallen – the firstborn, or wise
Councillor – prepared vistas extend
As far as harvest; and idyllic death
Where fish at dawn ignite the powdery lake.

King Log

Ovid in the Third Reich

non peccat, quaecumque potest peccasse negare,
solaque famosam culpa professa facit.
(AMORES, III, XIV)

I love my work and my children. God
Is distant, difficult. Things happen.
Too near the ancient troughs of blood
Innocence is no earthly weapon.

I have learned one thing: not to look down
So much upon the damned. They, in their sphere,
Harmonize strangely with the divine
Love. I, in mine, celebrate the love-choir.

Annunciations

The Word has been abroad, is back, with a tanned look
From its subsistence in the stiffening-mire.
Cleansing has become killing, the reward
Touchable, overt, clean to the touch.
Now at a distance from the steam of beasts,
The loathly neckings and fat shook spawn
(Each specimen-jar fed with delicate spawn)
The searchers with the curers sit at meat
And are satisfied. Such precious things put down
And the flesh eased through turbulence the soul
Purples itself; each eye squats full and mild
While all who attend to fiddle or to harp
For betterment, flavour their decent mouths
With gobbets of the sweetest sacrifice.

2

O Love, subject of the mere diurnal grind,
Forever being pledged to be redeemed,
Expose yourself for charity; be assured
The body is but husk and excrement.
Enter these deaths according to the law,
O visited women, possessed sons. Foreign lusts
Infringe our restraints; the changeable
Soldiery have their goings-out and comings-in
Dying in abundance. Choicest beasts
Suffuse the gutters with their colourful blood.
Our God scatters corruption. Priests, martyrs,
Parade to this imperious theme: 'O Love,
You know what pains succeed; be vigilant; strive
To recognize the damned among your friends.'

Locust Songs

To Allan Seager

THE EMBLEM

So with sweet oaths converting the salt earth
To yield, our fathers verged on Paradise:
Each to his own portion of Paradise,
Stung by the innocent venoms of the earth.

GOOD HUSBANDRY

Out of the foliage of sensual pride
Those teeming apples. Summer burned well
The dramatic flesh; made work for pride
Forking into the tender mouths of Hell

Heaped windfalls, pulp for the Gadarene
Squealers. This must be our reward:
To smell God writhing over the rich scene.
Gluttons for wrath, we stomach our reward.

SHILOH CHURCH, 1862:
TWENTY-THREE THOUSAND

O stamping-ground of the shod Word! So hard
On the heels of the damned red-man we came,
Geneva's tribe, outlandish and abhorred –
Bland vistas milky with Jehovah's calm –

Who fell to feasting Nature, the glare
Of buzzards circling; cried to the grim sun
'Jehovah punish us!'; who went too far;
In deserts dropped the odd white turds of bone;

Whose passion was to find out God in this
His natural filth, voyeur of sacrifice, a slow
Bloody unearthing of the God-in-us.
But with what blood, and to what end, Shiloh?

September Song

born 19.6.32 – deported 24.9.42

Undesirable you may have been, untouchable
you were not. Not forgotten
or passed over at the proper time.

As estimated, you died. Things marched,
sufficient, to that end.
Just so much Zyklon and leather, patented
terror, so many routine cries.

(I have made
an elegy for myself it
is true)

September fattens on vines. Roses
flake from the wall. The smoke
of harmless fires drifts to my eyes.

This is plenty. This is more than enough.

The Humanist

The *Venice* portrait; he
Broods, the achieved guest
Tired and word-perfect
At the Muses' table.

Virtue is virtù. These
Lips debate and praise
Some rich aphorism,
A delicate white meat.

The commonplace hands once
Thick with Plato's blood
(Tasteless! tasteless!) are laid
Dryly against the robes.

Funeral Music

William de la Pole, Duke of Suffolk: beheaded 1450
John Tiptoft, Earl of Worcester: beheaded 1470
Anthony Woodville, Earl Rivers: beheaded 1483

1

Processionals in the exemplary cave,
Benediction of shadows. Pomfret. London.
The voice fragrant with mannered humility,
With an equable contempt for this world,
'In honorem Trinitatis'. Crash. The head
Struck down into a meaty conduit of blood.
So these dispose themselves to receive each
Pentecostal blow from axe or seraph,
Spattering block-straw with mortal residue.
Psalteries whine through the empyrean. Fire
Flares in the pit, ghosting upon stone
Creatures of such rampant state, vacuous
Ceremony of possession, restless
Habitation, no man's dwelling-place.

2

For whom do we scrape our tribute of pain –
For none but the ritual king? We meditate
A rueful mystery; we are dying
To satisfy fat Caritas, those
Wiped jaws of stone. (Suppose all reconciled
By silent music; imagine the future
Flashed back at us, like steel against sun,
Ultimate recompense.) Recall the cold
Of Towton on Palm Sunday before dawn,
Wakefield, Tewkesbury; fastidious trumpets
Shrilling into the ruck; some trampled
Acres, parched, sodden or blanched by sleet,
Stuck with strange-postured dead. Recall the wind's
Flurrying, darkness over the human mire.

3

They bespoke doomsday and they meant it by
God, their curved metal rimming the low ridge.
But few appearances are like this. Once
Every five hundred years a comet's
Over-riding stillness might reveal men
In such array, livid and featureless,
With England crouched beastwise beneath it all.
'Oh, that old northern business . . .' A field
After battle utters its own sound
Which is like nothing on earth, but is earth.
Blindly the questing snail, vulnerable
Mole emerge, blindly we lie down, blindly
Among carnage the most delicate souls
Tup in their marriage-blood, gasping 'Jesus'.

4

Let mind be more precious than soul; it will not
Endure. Soul grasps its price, begs its own peace,
Settles with tears and sweat, is possibly
Indestructible. That I can believe.
Though I would scorn the mere instinct of faith,
Expediency of assent, if I dared,
What I dare not is a waste history
Or void rule. Averroes, old heathen,
If only you had been right, if Intellect
Itself were absolute law, sufficient grace,
Our lives could be a myth of captivity
Which we might enter: an unpeopled region
Of ever new-fallen snow, a palace blazing
With perpetual silence as with torches.

5

As with torches we go, at wild Christmas,
When we revel in our atonement
Through thirty feasts of unction and slaughter,
What is that but the soul's winter sleep?
So many things rest under consummate
Justice as though trumpets purified law,
Spikenard were the real essence of remorse.
The sky gathers up darkness. When we chant
'Ora, ora pro nobis' it is not
Seraphs who descend to pity but ourselves.
Those righteously-accused those vengeful
Racked on articulate looms indulge us
With lingering shows of pain, a flagrant
Tenderness of the damned for their own flesh:

6

My little son, when you could command marvels
Without mercy, outstare the wearisome
Dragon of sleep, I rejoiced above all –
A stranger well-received in your kingdom.
On those pristine fields I saw humankind
As it was named by the Father; fabulous
Beasts rearing in stillness to be blessed.
The world's real cries reached there, turbulence
From remote storms, rumour of solitudes,
A composed mystery. And so it ends.
Some parch for what they were; others are made
Blind to all but one vision, their necessity
To be reconciled. I believe in my
Abandonment, since it is what I have.

7

'Prowess, vanity, mutual regard,
It seemed I stared at them, they at me.
That was the gorgon's true and mortal gaze:
Averted conscience turned against itself.'
A hawk and a hawk-shadow. 'At noon,
As the armies met, each mirrored the other;
Neither was outshone. So they flashed and vanished
And all that survived them was the stark ground
Of this pain. I made no sound, but once
I stiffened as though a remote cry
Had heralded my name. It was nothing . . .'
Reddish ice tinged the reeds; dislodged, a few
Feathers drifted across; carrion birds
Strutted upon the armour of the dead.

8

Not as we are but as we must appear,
Contractual ghosts of pity; not as we
Desire life but as they would have us live,
Set apart in timeless colloquy.
So it is required; so we bear witness,
Despite ourselves, to what is beyond us,
Each distant sphere of harmony forever
Poised, unanswerable. If it is without
Consequence when we vaunt and suffer, or
If it is not, all echoes are the same
In such eternity. Then tell me, love,
How that should comfort us – or anyone
Dragged half-unnerved out of this worldly place,
Crying to the end 'I have not finished'.

Four Poems Regarding the Endurance of Poets

MEN ARE A MOCKERY OF ANGELS

i.m. Tommaso Campanella, priest and poet

Some days a shadow through
The high window shares my
Prison. I watch a slug
Scale the glinting pit-side
Of its own slime. The cries
As they come are mine; then
God's: my justice, wounds, love,
Derisive light, bread, filth.

To lie here in my strange
Flesh while glutted Torment
Sleeps, stained with its prompt food,
Is a joy past all care
Of the world, for a time.
But we are commanded
To rise, when, in silence,
I would compose my voice.

A PRAYER TO THE SUN

i.m. Miguel Hernandez

i

Darkness
above all things
the Sun
makes
rise

ii

Vultures
salute their meat
at noon
(Hell is
silent)

iii

Blind Sun
our ravager
bless us
so that
we sleep

'DOMAINE PUBLIC'

i.m. Robert Desnos, died Terezin Camp, 1945

For reading I can recommend
   the Fathers. How they
cultivate the corrupting flesh:

toothsome contemplation: cleanly
   maggots churning spleen
to milk. For exercise, prolonged

suppression of much improper
   speech from proper tombs.
If the ground opens, should men's mouths

open also? 'I am nothing
   if not saved now!' or
'Christ, what a pantomime!' The days

of the week are seven pits. Look,
   Seigneur, again we
resurrect and the judges come.

TRISTIA: 1891–1938

A Valediction to Osip Mandelstam

Difficult friend, I would have preferred
You to them. The dead keep their sealed lives
And again I am too late. Too late
The salutes, dust-clouds and brazen cries.

Images rear from desolation
Like ruins upon a plain.
A few men glare at their hands; others
Grovel for food in the roadside field.

Tragedy has all under regard.
It will not touch us but it is there –
Flawless, insatiate – hard summer sky
Feasting on this, reaching its own end.

The Imaginative Life

Evasive souls, of whom the wise lose track,
Die in each night, who, with their day-tongues, sift
The waking-taste of manna or of blood:

The raw magi, part-barbarians,
Entranced by demons and desert frost,
By the irregular visions of a god,

Suffragans of the true seraphs. Lust
Writhes, is dumb savage and in their way
As a virulence natural to the earth.

Renewed glories batten on the poor bones;
Gargantuan mercies whetted by a scent
Of mortal sweat: as though the sleeping flesh

Adored by Furies, stirred, yawned, were driven
In mid-terror to purging and delight.
As though the dead had *Finis* on their brows.

The Assisi Fragments

To G. Wilson Knight

1

Lion and lioness, the mild
Inflammable beasts,
At their precise peril kept
Distance and repose –
And there the serpent
Innocently shone its head.

2

So the hawk had its pursuit. So Death
Opened its childish eyes. So the angels
Overcame Adam: he was defiled
By balm. Creator, and creature made
Of unnatural earth, he howled
To the raven *find me*; to the wolf
Eat, my brother, and to the fire *I am clean*.

History as Poetry

Poetry as salutation; taste
Of Pentecost's ashen feast. Blue wounds.
The tongue's atrocities. Poetry
Unearths from among the speechless dead

Lazarus mystified, common man
Of death. The lily rears its gouged face
From the provided loam. Fortunate
Auguries; whirrings; tarred golden dung:

'A resurgence' as they say. The old
Laurels wagging with the new: Selah!
Thus laudable the trodden bone thus
Unanswerable the knack of tongues.

Soliloquies

THE STONE MAN

To Charles Causley

Recall, now, the omens of childhood:
The nettle-clump and rank elder-tree;
The stones waiting in the mason's yard:

Half-recognized kingdom of the dead:
A deeper landscape lit by distant
Flashings from their journey. At nightfall

My father scuffed clay into the house.
He set his boots on the bleak iron
Of the hearth; ate, drank, unbuckled, slept.

I leaned to the lamp; the pallid moths
Clipped its glass, made an autumnal sound.
Words clawed my mind as though they had smelt

Revelation's flesh . . . So, with an ease
That is dreadful, I summon all back.
The sun bellows over its parched swarms.

What I lost was not a part of this.
The dark-blistered foxgloves, wet berries
Glinting from shadow, small ferns and stones,

Seem fragments, in the observing mind,
Of its ritual power. Old age
Singles them out as though by first-light,

As though a still-life, preserving some
Portion of the soul's feast, went with me
Everywhere, to be hung in strange rooms,

Loneliness being what it is. If
I knew the exact coin for tribute,
Defeat might be bought, processional

Silence gesture its tokens of earth
At my mouth: as in the great death-songs
Of Propertius (although he died young).

Three Baroque Meditations

Do words make up the majesty
Of man, and his justice
Between the stones and the void?

How they watch us, the demons
Plugging their dumb wounds! When
Exorcized they shrivel yet thrive.

An owl plunges to its tryst
With a field-mouse in the sharp night.
My fire squeals and lies still.

Minerva, receive this hard
Praise: I speak well of Death;
I confess to the priest in me;

I am shadowed by the wise bird
Of necessity, the lithe
Paradigm Sleep-and-Kill.

2

Anguish bloated by the replete scream.
Flesh of abnegation: the poem
Moves grudgingly to its extreme form,

Vulnerable, to the lamp's fierce head
Of well-trimmed light. In darkness outside,
Foxes and rain-sleeked stones and the dead –

Aliens of such a theme – endure
Until I could cry 'Death! Death!' as though
To exacerbate that suave power;

But refrain. For I am circumspect,
Lifting the spicy lid of my tact
To sniff at the myrrh. It is perfect

In its impalpable bitterness,
Scent of a further country where worse
Furies promenade and bask their claws.

So white I was, he would have me cry
  'Unclean!' murderously
To heal me with far-fetched blood.

I writhed to conceive of him.
I clawed to becalm him.
Some nights, I witnessed his face in sleep

And dreamed of my father's
House. (By day he professed languages –
  Disciplines of languages)

By day I cleansed my thin tongue
From its nightly prowl, its vixen-skill,
  His sacramental mouth

  That justified my flesh
And moved well among women
In nuances and imperatives.

This was the poet of a people's
  Love. I hated him. He weeps,
Solemnizing his loss.

from *The Songbook of Sebastian Arrurruz*

Sebastian Arrurruz: 1868–1922

I

Ten years without you. For so it happens.
Days make their steady progress, a routine
That is merciful and attracts nobody.

Already, like a disciplined scholar,
I piece fragments together, past conjecture
Establishing true sequences of pain;

For so it is proper to find value
In a bleak skill, as in the thing restored:
The long-lost words of choice and valediction.

COPLAS

i

'One cannot lose what one has not possessed.'
So much for that abrasive gem.
I can lose what I want. I want you.

ii

Oh my dear one, I shall grieve for you
For the rest of my life with slightly
Varying cadence, oh my dear one.

iii

Half-mocking the half-truth, I note
'The wild brevity of sensual love'.
I am shaken, even by that.

iv

It is to him I write, it is to her
I speak in contained silence. Will they be touched
By the unfamiliar passion between them?

3

What other men do with other women
Is for me neither orgy nor sacrament
Nor a language of foreign candour

But is mere occasion or chance distance
Out of which you might move and speak my name
As I speak yours, bargaining with sleep's

Miscellaneous gods for as much
As I can have: an alien landscape,
The dream where you are always to be found.

5

Love, oh my love, it will come
Sure enough. A storm
Broods over the dry earth all day.
At night the shutters throb in its downpour.

The metaphor holds; is a snug house.
You are outside, lost somewhere. I find myself
Devouring verses of stranger passion
And exile. The exact words

Are fed into my blank hunger for you.

POSTURES

I imagine, as I imagine us
Each time more stylized more lovingly
Detailed, that I am not myself
But someone I might have been: sexless,
Indulgent about art, relishing
Let us say the well-schooled
Postures of *St Anthony* or *St Jerome*,
Those peaceful hermaphrodite dreams
Through which the excess of memory
Pursues its own abstinence.

Roughly-silvered leaves that are the snow
On Ararat seen through those leaves.
The sun lays down a foliage of shade.

A drinking-fountain pulses its head
Two or three inches from the troughed stone.
An old woman sucks there, gripping the rim.

Why do I have to relive, even now,
Your mouth, and your hand running over me
Deft as a lizard, like a sinew of water?

II

Scarcely speaking: it becomes as a
Coolness between neighbours. Often
There is this orgy of sleep. I wake
To caress propriety with odd words
And enjoy abstinence in a vocation
Of now-almost-meaningless despair.

Mercian Hymns

I

King of the perennial holly-groves, the riven sandstone:
overlord of the M5: architect of the historic rampart
and ditch, the citadel at Tamworth, the summer her-
mitage in Holy Cross: guardian of the Welsh Bridge
and the Iron Bridge: contractor to the desirable new
estates: saltmaster: moneychanger: commissioner for
oaths: martyrologist: the friend of Charlemagne.

'I liked that,' said Offa, 'sing it again.'

II

A pet-name, a common name. Best-selling brand, curt
graffito. A laugh; a cough. A syndicate. A specious gift.
Scoffed-at horned phonograph.

The starting-cry of a race. A name to conjure with.

III

On the morning of the crowning we chorused our remission
from school. It was like Easter: hankies and gift-mugs
approved by his foreign gaze, the village-lintels curlered
with paper flags.

We gaped at the car-park of 'The Stag's Head' where a
bonfire of beer-crates and holly-boughs whistled above
the tar. And the chef stood there, a king in his new-risen
hat, sealing his brisk largesse with 'any mustard?'

IV

I was invested in mother-earth, the crypt of roots and end-
ings. Child's-play. I abode there, bided my time: where
the mole

shouldered the clogged wheel, his gold solidus; where
dry-dust badgers thronged the Roman flues, the long-
unlooked-for mansions of our tribe.

V

So much for the elves' wergild, the true governance of England, the gaunt warrior-gospel armoured in engraved stone. I wormed my way heavenward for ages amid barbaric ivy, scrollwork of fern.

Exile or pilgrim set me once more upon that ground: my rich and desolate childhood. Dreamy, smug-faced, sick on outings – I who was taken to be a king of some kind, a prodigy, a maimed one.

VI

The princes of Mercia were badger and raven. Thrall to
their freedom, I dug and hoarded. Orchards fruited
above clefts. I drank from honeycombs of chill sand-
stone.

'A boy at odds in the house, lonely among brothers.' But I,
who had none, fostered a strangeness; gave myself to
unattainable toys.

Candles of gnarled resin, apple-branches, the tacky mistle-
toe. 'Look' they said and again 'look.' But I ran slowly;
the landscape flowed away, back to its source.

In the schoolyard, in the cloakrooms, the children boasted
their scars of dried snot; wrists and knees garnished with
impetigo.

VII

Gasholders, russet among fields. Milldams, marlpools that lay unstirring. Eel-swarms. Coagulations of frogs: once, with branches and half-bricks, he battered a ditchful; then sidled away from the stillness and silence.

Ceolred was his friend and remained so, even after the day of the lost fighter: a biplane, already obsolete and irreplaceable, two inches of heavy snub silver. Ceolred let it spin through a hole in the classroom-floorboards, softly, into the rat-droppings and coins.

After school he lured Ceolred, who was sniggering with fright, down to the old quarries, and flayed him. Then, leaving Ceolred, he journeyed for hours, calm and alone, in his private derelict sandlorry named *Albion*.

VIII

The mad are predators. Too often lately they harbour
  against us. A novel heresy exculpates all maimed souls.
  Abjure it! I am the King of Mercia, and I know.

Threatened by phone-calls at midnight, venomous letters,
  forewarned I have thwarted their imminent devices.

Today I name them; tomorrow I shall express the new law.
  I dedicate my awakening to this matter.

IX

The strange church smelled a bit 'high', of censers and polish. The strange curate was just as appropriate: he took off into the marriage-service. No-one cared to challenge that gambit.

Then he dismissed you, and the rest of us followed, sheepish next-of-kin, to the place without the walls: spoil-heaps of chrysanths dead in their plastic macs, eldorado of washstand-marble.

Embarrassed, we dismissed ourselves: the three mute great-aunts borne away down St Chad's Garth in a stiff-backed Edwardian Rolls.

I unburden the saga of your burial, my dear. You had lived long enough to see things 'nicely settled'.

X

He adored the desk, its brown-oak inlaid with ebony,
assorted prize pens, the seals of gold and base metal into
which he had sunk his name.

It was there that he drew upon grievances from the people;
attended to signatures and retributions; forgave the
death-howls of his rival. And there he exchanged gifts
with the Muse of History.

What should a man make of remorse, that it might profit his
soul? Tell me. Tell everything to Mother, darling, and
God bless.

He swayed in sunlight, in mild dreams. He tested the little
pears. He smeared catmint on his palm for his cat Smut
to lick. He wept, attempting to master *ancilla* and *servus*.

XI

Coins handsome as Nero's; of good substance and weight. *Offa Rex* resonant in silver, and the names of his moneyers. They struck with accountable tact. They could alter the king's face.

Exactness of design was to deter imitation; mutilation if that failed. Exemplary metal, ripe for commerce. Value from a sparse people, scrapers of salt-pans and byres.

Swathed bodies in the long ditch; one eye upstaring. It is safe to presume, here, the king's anger. He reigned forty years. Seasons touched and retouched the soil.

Heathland, new-made watermeadow. Charlock, marsh-marigold. Crepitant oak forest where the boar furrowed black mould, his snout intimate with worms and leaves.

XII

Their spades grafted through the variably-resistant soil.
    They clove to the hoard. They ransacked epiphanies,
    vertebrae of the chimera, armour of wild bees' larvae.
    They struck the fire-dragon's faceted skin.

The men were paid to caulk water-pipes. They brewed and
    pissed amid splendour; their latrine seethed its estuary
    through nettles. They are scattered to your collations,
    moldywarp.

It is autumn. Chestnut-boughs clash their inflamed leaves.
    The garden festers for attention: telluric cultures enriched
    with shards, corms, nodules, the sunk solids of gravity.
    I have raked up a golden and stinking blaze.

XIII

Trim the lamp; polish the lens; draw, one by one, rare coins to the light. Ringed by its own lustre, the masterful head emerges, kempt and jutting, out of England's well. Far from his underkingdom of crinoid and crayfish, the rune-stone's province, *Rex Totius Anglorum Patriae*, coiffured and ageless, portrays the self-possession of his possession, cushioned on a legend.

XIV

Dismissing reports and men, he put pressure on the wax, blistered it to a crest. He threatened malefactors with ash from his noon cigar.

When the sky cleared above Malvern, he lingered in his orchard; by the quiet hammer-pond. Trout-fry simmered there, translucent, as though forming the water's under-skin. He had a care for natural minutiae. What his gaze touched was his tenderness. Woodlice sat pellet-like in the cracked bark and a snail sugared its new stone.

At dinner, he relished the mockery of drinking his family's health. He did this whenever it suited him, which was not often.

XV

Tutting, he wrenched at a snarled root of dead crabapple.
It rose against him. In brief cavort he was Cernunnos, the
branched god, lightly concussed.

He divided his realm. It lay there like a dream. An ancient
land, full of strategy. Ramparts of compost pioneered
by red-helmeted worms. Hemlock in ambush, night-soil,
tetanus. A wasps' nest ensconced in the hedge-bank,
a reliquary or wrapped head, the corpse of Cernunnos
pitching dayward its feral horns.

XVI

Clash of salutation. As keels thrust into shingle. Ambas-
sadors, pilgrims. What is carried over? The Frankish gift,
two-edged, regaled with slaughter.

The sword is in the king's hands; the crux a craftsman's
triumph. Metal effusing its own fragrance, a variety of
balm. And other miracles, other exchanges.

Shafts from the winter sun homing upon earth's rim.
Christ's mass: in the thick of a snowy forest the flickering
evergreen fissured with light.

Attributes assumed, retribution entertained. What is borne
amongst them? Too much or too little. Indulgences of
bartered acclaim; an expenditure, a hissing. Wine, urine
and ashes.

XVII

He drove at evening through the hushed Vosges. The car
radio, glimmering, received broken utterance from the
horizon of storms . . .

'God's honour – our bikes touched; he skidded and came
off.' 'Liar.' A timid father's protective bellow. Disfigure-
ment of a village-king. 'Just look at the bugger . . .'

His maroon GT chanted then overtook. He lavished on the
high valleys its *haleine*.

XVIII

At Pavia, a visitation of some sorrow. Boethius' dungeon.
He shut his eyes, gave rise to a tower out of the earth.
He willed the instruments of violence to break upon
meditation. Iron buckles gagged; flesh leaked rennet over
them; the men stooped, disentangled the body.

He wiped his lips and hands. He strolled back to the car,
with discreet souvenirs for consolation and philosophy.
He set in motion the furtherance of his journey. To
watch the Tiber foaming out much blood.

XIX

Behind the thorn-trees thin smoke, scutch-grass or wattle
smouldering. At this distance it is hard to tell. Far cries
impinge like the faint tinking of iron.

We have a kitchen-garden riddled with toy-shards, with
splinters of habitation. The children shriek and scavenge,
play havoc. They incinerate boxes, rags and old tyres.
They haul a sodden log, hung with soft shields of fungus,
and launch it upon the flames.

XX

Primeval heathland spattered with the bones of mice and
birds; where adders basked and bees made provision,
mantling the inner walls of their burh:

Coiled entrenched England: brickwork and paintwork
stalwart above hacked marl. The clashing primary
colours – 'Ethandune', 'Catraeth', 'Maldon', 'Pengwern'.
Steel against yew and privet. Fresh dynasties of smiths.

XXI

Cohorts of charabancs fanfared Offa's province and his con-
cern, negotiating the by-ways from Teme to Trent. Their
windshields dripped butterflies. Stranded on hilltops they
signalled with plumes of steam. Twilight menaced the
land. The young women wept and surrendered.

Still, everyone was cheerful, heedless in such days: at
summer weekends dipping into valleys beyond Mercia's
dyke. Tea was enjoyed, by lakesides where all might
fancy carillons of real Camelot vibrating through the
silent water.

Gradually, during the years, deciduous velvet peeled from
evergreen albums and during the years more treasures
were mislaid: the harp-shaped brooches, the nuggets of
fool's gold.

XXII

We ran across the meadow scabbed with cow-dung, past the crab-apple trees and camouflaged nissen hut. It was curfew-time for our war-band.

At home the curtains were drawn. The wireless boomed its commands. I loved the battle-anthems and the gregarious news.

Then, in the earthy shelter, warmed by a blue-glassed storm-lantern, I huddled with stories of dragon-tailed airships and warriors who took wing immortal as phantoms.

XXIII

In tapestries, in dreams, they gathered, as it was enacted, the
  return, the re-entry of transcendence into this sublunary
  world. *Opus Anglicanum*, their stringent mystery riddled
  by needles: the silver veining, the gold leaf, voluted grape-
  vine, master-works of treacherous thread.

They trudged out of the dark, scraping their boots free from
  lime-splodges and phlegm. They munched cold bacon.
  The lamps grew plump with oily reliable light.

XXIV

Itinerant through numerous domains, of his lord's retinue,
to Compostela. Then home for a lifetime amid West
Mercia this master-mason as I envisage him, intent to
pester upon tympanum and chancel-arch his moody
testament, confusing warrior with lion, dragon-coils,
tendrils of the stony vine.

Where best to stand? Easter sunrays catch the oblique
face of Adam scrumping through leaves; pale spree of
evangelists and, there, a cross Christ mumming child
Adam out of Hell

('Et exspecto resurrectionem mortuorum' dust in the eyes,
on clawing wings, and lips)

XXV

Brooding on the eightieth letter of *Fors Clavigera*, I speak
  this in memory of my grandmother, whose childhood
  and prime womanhood were spent in the nailer's darg.

The nailshop stood back of the cottage, by the fold. It
  reeked stale mineral sweat. Sparks had furred its low
  roof. In dawn-light the troughed water floated a damson-
  bloom of dust –

not to be shaken by posthumous clamour. It is one thing
  to celebrate the 'quick forge', another to cradle a face
  hare-lipped by the searing wire.

Brooding on the eightieth letter of *Fors Clavigera*, I speak
  this in memory of my grandmother, whose childhood
  and prime womanhood were spent in the nailer's darg.

XXVI

Fortified in their front parlours, at Yuletide men are the
more murderous. Drunk, they defy battle-axes, bellow of
whale-bone and dung.

Troll-wives, groaners in sweetness, tooth-bewitchers, you
too must purge for the surfeit of England – who have
scattered peppermint and confetti, your hundreds-and-
thousands.

XXVII

'Now when King Offa was alive and dead', they were all there, the funereal gleemen: papal legate and rural dean; Merovingian car-dealers, Welsh mercenaries; a shuffle of house-carls.

He was defunct. They were perfunctory. The ceremony stood acclaimed. The mob received memorial vouchers and signs.

After that shadowy, thrashing midsummer hail-storm, Earth lay for a while, the ghost-bride of livid Thor, butcher of strawberries, and the shire-tree dripped red in the arena of its uprooting.

XXVIII

Processes of generation; deeds of settlement. The urge to marry well; wit to invest in the properties of healing-springs. Our children and our children's children, o my masters.

Tracks of ancient occupation. Frail ironworks rusting in the thorn-thicket. Hearthstones; charred lullabies. A solitary axe-blow that is the echo of a lost sound.

Tumult recedes as though into the long rain. Groves of legendary holly; silverdark the ridged gleam.

XXIX

'Not strangeness, but strange likeness. Obstinate, outclassed
forefathers, I too concede, I am your staggeringly-gifted
child.'

So, murmurous, he withdrew from them. Gran lit the gas,
his dice whirred in the ludo-cup, he entered into the last
dream of Offa the King.

XXX

And it seemed, while we waited, he began to walk towards
   us   he vanished

he left behind coins, for his lodging, and traces of red mud.

Tenebrae

The Pentecost Castle

It is terrible to desire and not
possess, and terrible to possess
and not desire.

W. B. YEATS

What we love in other human
beings is the hoped-for satisfaction
of our desire. We do not love their
desire. If what we loved in them
was their desire, then we should
love them as ourself.

SIMONE WEIL

1

They slew by night
upon the road
Medina's pride
Olmedo's flower

shadows warned him
not to go
not to go
along that road

weep for your lord
Medina's pride
Olmedo's flower
there in the road

2

Down in the orchard
I met my death
under the briar rose
I lie slain

I was going
to gather flowers
my love waited
among the trees

down in the orchard
I met my death
under the briar rose
I lie slain

3

You watchers on the wall
grown old with care
I too looked from the wall
I shall look no more

tell us what you saw
the lord I sought to serve
caught in the thorn grove
his blood on his brow

you keepers of the wall
what friend or enemy
sets free the cry
of the bell

4

At dawn the Mass
burgeons from stone
a Jesse tree
of resurrection

budding with candle
flames the gold
and the white wafers
of the feast

and ghosts for love
void a few tears
of wax upon
forlorn altars

5

Goldfinch and hawk
and the grey aspen tree
I have run to the river
mother call me home

the leaves glint in the wind
turning their quiet song
the wings flash and are still
I sleep in the shade

when I cried out you
made no reply
tonight I shall pass by
without a sound

6

Slowly my heron flies
pierced by the blade
mounting in slow pain
strikes the air with its cries

goes seeking the high rocks
where no man can climb
where the wild balsam stirs
by the little stream

the rocks the high rocks
are brimming with flowers
there love grows and there love
rests and is saved

7

I went out early
to the far field
ermine and lily
and yet a child

Love stood before me
in that place
prayers could not lure me
to Christ's house

Christ the deceiver
took all I had
his darkness ever
my fair reward

8

And you my spent heart's treasure
my yet unspent desire
measurer past all measure
cold paradox of fire

as seeker so forsaken
consentingly denied
your solitude a token
the sentries at your side

fulfilment to my sorrow
indulgence of your prey
the sparrowhawk the sparrow
the nothing that you say

9

This love will see me dead
he has the place in mind
where I am free to die
be true at last true love

my love meet me half-way
I bear no sword of fear
where you dwell I
dwell also says my lord

dealing his five wounds
so cunning and so true
of love to rouse this death
I die to sleep in love

St James and St John
bless the road she has gone
St John and St James
a rosary of names

child-beads of fingered bread
never-depleted heart's food
the nominal the real
subsistence past recall

bread we shall never break
love-runes we cannot speak
scrolled effigy of a cry
our passion its display

If the night is dark
and the way short
if the way you take
is to my heart

say though I never
see you again
touch me I shall shiver
at the unseen

the night is so dark
the way so short
yet you do not wake
against my heart

12

Married and not for love
you of all women
you of all women
my soul's darling my love

faithful to my desire
lost in the dream's grasp where
shall I find you everywhere
unmatched in my desire

each of us dispossessed
so richly in my sleep
I rise out of my sleep
crying like one possessed

13

Splendidly-shining darkness
proud citadel of meekness
likening us our unlikeness
majesty of our distress

emptiness ever thronging
untenable belonging
how long until this longing
end in unending song

and soul for soul discover
no strangeness to dissever
and lover keep with lover
a moment and for ever

14

As he is wounded
I am hurt
he bleeds from pride
I from my heart

as he is dying
I shall live
in grief desiring
still to grieve

as he is living
I shall die
sick of forgiving
such honesty

15

I shall go down
to the lovers' well
and wash this wound
that will not heal

beloved soul
what shall you see
nothing at all
yet eye to eye

depths of non-being
perhaps too clear
my desire dying
as I desire

from *Lachrimae*

MARTYRIUM

The Jesus-faced man walking crowned with flies
who swats the roadside grass or glances up
at the streaked gibbet with its birds that swoop,
who scans his breviary while the sweat dries,

fades, now, among the fading tapestries,
brooches of crimson tears where no eyes weep,
a mouth unstitched into a rimless cup,
torn clouds the cauldrons of the martyrs' cries.

Clamorous love, its faint and baffled shout,
its grief that would betray him to our fear,
he suffers for our sake, or does not hear

above the hiss of shadows on the wheat.
Viaticum transfigures earth's desire
in rising vernicles of summer air.

PAVANA DOLOROSA

Loves I allow and passions I approve:
Ash-Wednesday feasts, ascetic opulence,
the wincing lute, so real in its pretence,
itself a passion amorous of love.

Self-wounding martyrdom, what joys you have,
true-torn among this fictive consonance,
music's creation of the moveless dance,
the decreation to which all must move.

Self-seeking hunter of forms, there is no end
to such pursuits. None can revoke your cry.
Your silence is an ecstasy of sound

and your nocturnals blaze upon the day.
I founder in desire for things unfound.
I stay amid the things that will not stay.

Crucified Lord, so naked to the world,
you live unseen within that nakedness,
consigned by proxy to the judas-kiss
of our devotion, bowed beneath the gold,

with re-enactments, penances foretold:
scentings of love across a wilderness
of retrospection, wild and objectless
longings incarnate in the carnal child.

Beautiful for themselves the icons fade;
the lions and the hermits disappear.
Triumphalism feasts on empty dread,

fulfilling triumphs of the festal year.
We find you wounded by the token spear.
Dominion is swallowed with your blood.

from *An Apology for the Revival of Christian Architecture in England*

the spiritual, Platonic old England . . .
s. t. coleridge, *Anima Poetae*

'Your situation', said Coningsby, looking up the green
and silent valley, 'is absolutely poetic.'
'I try sometimes to fancy', said Mr Millbank, with a
rather fierce smile, 'that I am in the New World.'
benjamin disraeli, *Coningsby*

QUAINT MAZES

And, after all, it is to them we return.
Their triumph is to rise and be our hosts:
lords of unquiet or of quiet sojourn,
those muddy-hued and midge-tormented ghosts.

On blustery lilac-bush and terrace-urn
bedaubed with bloom Linnaean pentecosts
put their pronged light; the chilly fountains burn.
Religion of the heart, with trysts and quests

and pangs of consolation, its hawk's hood
twitched off for sweet carnality, again
rejoices in old hymns of servitude,

haunting the sacred well, the hidden shrine.
It is the ravage of the heron wood;
it is the rood blazing upon the green.

DAMON'S LAMENT FOR HIS CLORINDA, YORKSHIRE 1654

November rips gold foil from the oak ridges.
Dour folk huddle in High Hoyland, Penistone.
The tributaries of the Sheaf and Don
bulge their dull spate, cramming the poor bridges.

The North Sea batters our shepherds' cottages
from sixty miles. No sooner has the sun
swung clear above earth's rim than it is gone,
We live like gleaners of its vestiges

knowing we flourish, though each year a child
with the set face of a tomb-weeper is put down
for ever and ever. Why does the air grow cold

in the region of mirrors? And who is this clown
doffing his mask at the masked threshold
to selfless raptures that are all his own?

Make miniatures of the once-monstrous theme:
the red-coat devotees, mêlées of wheels,
Jagannath's lovers. With indifferent aim
unleash the rutting cannon at the walls

of forts and palaces; pollute the wells.
Impound the memoirs for their bankrupt shame,
fantasies of true destiny that kills
'under the sanction of the English name'.

Be moved by faith, obedience without fault,
the flawless hubris of heroic guilt,
the grace of visitation; and be stirred

by all her god-quests, her idolatries,
in conclave of abiding injuries,
sated upon the stillness of the bride.

Suppose they sweltered here three thousand years
patient for our destruction. There is a greeting
beyond the act. Destiny is the great thing,
true lord of annexation and arrears.

Our law-books overrule the emperors.
The mango is the bride-bed of light. Spring
jostles the flame-tree. But new mandates bring
new images of faith, good subahdars!

The flittering candles of the wayside shrines
melt into dawn. The sun surmounts the dust.
Krishna from Radha lovingly untwines.

Lugging the earth, the oxen bow their heads.
The alien conscience of our days is lost
among the ruins and on endless roads.

Malcolm and Frere, Colebrooke and Elphinstone,
the life of empire like the life of the mind
'simple, sensuous, passionate', attuned
to the clear theme of justice and order, gone.

Gone the ascetic pastimes, the Persian
scholarship, the wild boar run to ground,
the watercolours of the sun and wind.
Names rise like outcrops on the rich terrain,

like carapaces of the Mughal tombs
lop-sided in the rice-fields, boarded-up
near railway-crossings and small aerodromes.

'India's a peacock-shrine next to a shop
selling mangola, sitars, lucky charms,
heavenly Buddhas smiling in their sleep.'

LOSS AND GAIN

Pitched high above the shallows of the sea
lone bells in gritty belfries do not ring
but coil a far and inward echoing
out of the air that thrums. Enduringly,

fuchsia-hedges fend between cliff and sky;
brown stumps of headstones tamp into the ling
the ruined and the ruinously strong.
Platonic England grasps its tenantry

where wild-eyed poppies raddle tawny farms
and wild swans root in lily-clouded lakes.
Vulnerable to each other the twin forms

of sleep and waking touch the man who wakes
to sudden light, who thinks that this becalms
even the phantoms of untold mistakes.

THE LAUREL AXE

Autumn resumes the land, ruffles the woods
with smoky wings, entangles them. Trees shine
out from their leaves, rocks mildew to moss-green;
the avenues are spread with brittle floods.

Platonic England, house of solitudes,
rests in its laurels and its injured stone,
replete with complex fortunes that are gone,
beset by dynasties of moods and clouds.

It stands, as though at ease with its own world,
the mannerly extortions, languid praise,
all that devotion long since bought and sold,

the rooms of cedar and soft-thudding baize,
tremulous boudoirs where the crystals kissed
in cabinets of amethyst and frost.

Remember how, at seven years, the decrees
were brought home: child-soul must register
for Christ's dole, be allotted its first Easter,
blanch-white and empty, chilled by the lilies,

betrothed among the well-wishers and spies.
Reverend Mother, breakfastless, could feast her
constraint on terracotta and alabaster
and brimstone and the sweets of paradise.

Theology makes good bedside reading. Some
who are lost covet scholastic proof,
subsistence of probation, modest balm.

The wooden wings of justice borne aloof,
we close our eyes to Anselm and lie calm.
All night the cisterns whisper in the roof.

THE HEREFORDSHIRE CAROL

So to celebrate that kingdom: it grows
greener in winter, essence of the year;
the apple-branches musty with green fur.
In the viridian darkness of its yews

it is an enclave of perpetual vows
broken in time. Its truth shows disrepair,
disfigured shrines, their stones of gossamer,
Old Moore's astrology, all hallows,

the squire's effigy bewigged with frost,
and hobnails cracking puddles before dawn.
In grange and cottage girls rise from their beds

by candlelight and mend their ruined braids.
Touched by the cry of the iconoclast,
how the rose-window blossoms with the sun!

Two Chorale-Preludes
on melodies by Paul Celan

I AVE REGINA COELORUM

Es ist ein Land Verloren . . .

There is a land called Lost
at peace inside our heads.
The moon, full on the frost,
vivifies these stone heads.

Moods of the verb 'to stare',
split selfhoods, conjugate
ice-facets from the air,
the light glazing the light.

Look at us, Queen of Heaven.
Our solitudes drift by
your solitudes, the seven
dead stars in your sky.

2 TE LUCIS ANTE TERMINUM

Wir gehen dir, Heimat, ins Garn . . .

Centaury with your staunch bloom
you there alder beech you fern,
midsummer closeness my far home,
fresh traces of lost origin.

Silvery the black cherries hang,
the plum-tree oozes through each cleft
and horse-flies siphon the green dung,
glued to the sweetness of their graft:

immortal transience, a 'kind
of otherness', self-understood,
BE FAITHFUL grows upon the mind
as lichen glimmers on the wood.

A Pre-Raphaelite Notebook

Primroses; salutations; the miry skull
of a half-eaten ram; viscous wounds in earth
opening. What seraphs are afoot.

Gold seraph to gold worm in the pierced slime:
greetings. Advent of power-in-grace. The power
of flies distracts the working of our souls.

Earth's abundance. The God-ejected Word
resorts to flesh, procures carrion, satisfies
its white hunger. Salvation's travesty

a deathless metaphor: the stale head
sauced in original blood; the little feast
foaming with cries of rapture and despair.

Terribilis Est Locus Iste
Gauguin and the Pont-Aven School

Briefly they are amazed. The marigold-fields
mell and shudder and the travellers,
in sudden exile burdened with remote
hieratic gestures, journey to no end

beyond the vivid severance of each day,
strangeness at doors, a different solitude
between the mirror and the window, marked
visible absences, colours of the mind,

marginal angels lightning-sketched in red
chalk on the month's accounts or marigolds
in paint runnily embossed, or the renounced
self-portrait with a seraph and a storm.

Veni Coronaberis

A Garland for Helen Waddell

The crocus armies from the dead
rise up; the realm of love renews
the battle it was born to lose,
though for a time the snows have fled

and old stones blossom in the south
with sculpted vine and psaltery
and half-effaced adultery
the bird-dung dribbling from its mouth;

and abstinence crowns all our care
with martyr-laurels for this day.
Towers and steeples rise away
into the towering gulfs of air.

'Christmas Trees'

Bonhoeffer in his skylit cell
bleached by the flares' candescent fall,
pacing out his own citadel,

restores the broken themes of praise,
encourages our borrowed days,
by logic of his sacrifice.

Against wild reasons of the state
his words are quiet but not too quiet.
We hear too late or not too late.

*The Mystery of the Charity
of Charles Péguy*

Crack of a starting-pistol. Jean Jaurès
dies in a wine-puddle. Who or what stares
through the café-window crêped in powder-smoke?
The bill for the new farce reads *Sleepers Awake*.

History commands the stage wielding a toy gun,
rehearsing another scene. It has raged so before,
countless times; and will do, countless times more,
in the guise of supreme clown, dire tragedian.

In Brutus' name martyr and mountebank
ghost Caesar's ghost, his wounds of air and ink
painlessly spouting. Jaurès' blood lies stiff
on menu-card, shirt-front and handkerchief.

Did Péguy kill Jaurès? Did he incite
the assassin? Must men stand by what they write
as by their camp-beds or their weaponry
or shell-shocked comrades while they sag and cry?

Would Péguy answer – stubbornly on guard
among the *Cahiers*, with his army cape
and steely pince-nez and his hermit's beard,
brooding on conscience and embattled hope?

Truth's pedagogue, braving an entrenched class
of fools and scoundrels, children of the world,
his eyes caged and hostile behind glass –
still Péguy said that Hope is a little child.

Violent contrariety of men and days; calm
juddery bombardment of a silent film
showing such things: its canvas slashed with rain
and St Elmo's fire. Victory of the machine!

The brisk celluloid clatters through the gate;
the cortège of the century dances in the street;
and over and over the jolly cartoon
armies of France go reeling towards Verdun.

2

Rage and regret are tireless to explain
stratagems of the out-manoeuvred man,
the charge and counter-charge. You know the drill,
raw veteran, poet with the head of a bull.

Footslogger of genius, skirmisher with grace
and ill-luck, sentinel of the sacrifice,
without vantage of vanity, though mortal-proud,
defend your first position to the last word.

The sun-tanned earth is your centurion;
you are its tribune. On the hard-won
high places the old soldiers of old France
crowd like good children wrapped in obedience

and sleep, and ready to be taken home.
Whatever that vision, it is not a child's;
it is what a child's vision can become.
Memory, Imagination, harvesters of those fields,

our gifts are spoils, our virtues epitaphs,
our substance is the grass upon the graves.
'Du calme, mon vieux, du calme.' How studiously
one cultivates the sugars of decay,

pâtisserie-tinklings of angels ' 'sieur-'dame',
the smile of the dead novice in its plush frame,
while greed and disaffection are ingrained
like chalk-dust in the ranklings of the mind.

'Rather the Marne than the *Cahiers*.' True enough,
you took yourself off. Dying, your whole life
fell into place. ' 'Sieurs-'dames, this is the wall
where he leaned and rested, this is the well

from which he drank.' Péguy, you mock us now.
History takes the measure of your brow
in blank-eyed bronze, brave mediocre work
of *Niclausse, sculpteur*, cornered in the park

among the stout dogs and lame patriots
and all those ghosts, far-gazing in mid-stride,
rising from where they fell, still on parade,
covered in glory and the blood of beetroots.

3

Vistas of richness and reward. The cedar
uprears its lawns of black cirrus. You have found
hundred-fold return though in the land
of exile. You are Joseph the Provider;

and in the fable this is your proper home;
three sides of a courtyard where the bees thrum
in the crimped hedges and the pigeons flirt
and paddle, and sunlight pierces the heart-

shaped shutter-patterns in the afternoon,
shadows of fleurs-de-lys on the stone floors.
Here life is labour and pastime and orison
like something from a simple book of hours;

and immortality, your measured task,
inscribes its antique scars on the new desk
among your relics, bits of ivory quartz
and dented snuffbox won at Austerlitz.

The proofs pile up; the dead are made alive
to their posthumous fame. Here is the archive
of your stewardship; here is your true domaine,
its fields of discourse ripening to the Marne.

Chateau de Trie is yours, Chartres is yours,
and the carved knight of Gisors with the hound;
Colombey-les-deux-Eglises; St Cyr's
cadres and echelons are yours to command.

Yours is their dream of France, militant-pastoral:
musky red gillyvors, the wicker bark
of clematis braided across old brick
and the slow chain that cranks out of the well

morning and evening. It is Domrémy
restored; the mystic strategy of Foch
and Bergson with its time-scent, dour panache
deserving of martyrdom. It is an army

of poets, converts, vine-dressers, men skilled
in wood or metal, peasants from the Beauce,
terse teachers of Latin and those unschooled
in all but the hard rudiments of grace.

Such dreams portend, the dreamer prophesies,
is this not true? Truly, if you are wise,
deny such wisdom; bid the grim bonne-femme
defend your door: 'M'sieur is not at home.'

4

This world is different, belongs to them –
the lords of limit and of contumely.
It matters little whether you go tamely
or with rage and defiance to your doom.

This is your enemies' country which they took
in the small hours an age before you woke,
went to the window, saw the mist-hewn
statues of the lean kine emerge at dawn.

Outflanked again, too bad! You still have pride,
haggard obliquities: those that take remorse
and the contempt of others for a muse,
bound to the alexandrine as to the *Code*

Napoléon. Thus the bereaved soul returns
upon itself, grows resolute at chess,
in war-games hurling dice of immense loss
into the breach; thus punitively mourns.

This is no old Beauce manoir that you keep
but the rue de la Sorbonne, the cramped shop,
its unsold *Cahiers* built like barricades,
its fierce disciples, disciplines and feuds,

the camelot-cry of 'sticks!' As Tharaud says,
'all through your life the sound of broken glass.'
So much for Jaurès murdered in cold pique
by some vexed shadow of the belle époque,

some guignol strutting at the window-frame.
But what of you, Péguy, who came to 'exult',
to be called 'wolfish' by your friends? The guilt
belongs to time; and you must leave on time.

Jaurès was killed blindly, yet with reason:
'let us have drums to beat down his great voice.'
So you spoke to the blood. So, you have risen
above all that and fallen flat on your face

among the beetroots, where we are constrained
to leave you sleeping and to step aside
from the fleshed bayonets, the fusillade
of red-rimmed smoke like stubble being burned;

to turn away and contemplate the working
of the radical soul – instinct, intelligence,
memory, call it what you will – waking
into the foreboding of its inheritance,

its landscape and inner domain; images
of earth and grace. Across Artois the rois-mages
march on Bethlehem; sun-showers fall
slantwise over the kalefield, the canal.

Hedgers and ditchers, quarrymen, thick-shod
curés de campagne, each with his load,
shake off those cares and burdens; they become,
in a bleak visionary instant, seraphim

looking towards Chartres, the spired sheaves,
stone-thronged annunciations, winged ogives
uplifted and uplifting from the winter-gleaned
furrows of that criss-cross-trodden ground.

Or say it is Pentecost: the hawthorn-tree,
set with coagulate magnified flowers of may,
blooms in a haze of light; old chalk-pits brim
with seminal verdure from the roots of time.

Landscape is like revelation; it is both
singular crystal and the remotest things.
Cloud-shadows of seasons revisit the earth,
odourless myrrh borne by the wandering kings.

Happy are they who, under the gaze of God,
die for the 'terre charnelle', marry her blood
to theirs, and, in strange Christian hope, go down
into the darkness of resurrection,

into sap, ragwort, melancholy thistle,
almondy meadowsweet, the freshet-brook
rising and running through small wilds of oak,
past the elder-tump that is the child's castle.

Inevitable high summer, richly scarred
with furze and grief; winds drumming the fame
of the tin legions lost in haystack and stream.
Here the lost are blest, the scarred most sacred:

odd village workshops grimed and peppercorned
in a dust of dead spiders, paper-crowned
sunflowers with the bleached heads of rag dolls,
brushes in aspic, clay pots, twisted nails;

the clinking anvil and clear sheepbell-sound,
at noon and evening, of the angelus;
coifed girls like geese, labourers cap in hand,
and walled gardens espaliered with angels;

solitary bookish ecstasies, proud tears,
proud tears, for the forlorn hope, the guerdon
of Sedan, 'oh les braves gens!', English Gordon
stepping down sedately into the spears.

Patience hardens to a pittance, courage
unflinchingly declines into sour rage,
the cobweb-banners, the shrill bugle-bands
and the bronze warriors resting on their wounds.

These fatal decencies, they make us lords
over ourselves: familial debts and dreads,
keepers of old scores, the kindly ones
telling their beady sous, the child-eyed crones

who guard the votive candles and the faint
invalid's night-light of the sacrament,
a host of lilies and the table laid
for early mass from which you stood aside

to find salvation, your novena cleaving
brusquely against the grain of its own myth,
its truth and justice, to a kind of truth,
a justice hard to justify. 'Having

spoken his mind he'd a mind to be silent.'
But who would credit that, that one talent
dug from the claggy Beauce and returned to it
with love, honour, suchlike bitter fruit?

6

To dispense, with justice; or, to dispense
with justice. Thus the catholic god of France,
with honours all even, honours all, even
the damned in the brazen Invalides of Heaven.

Here there should be a section without words
for military band alone: 'Sambre et Meuse',
the 'Sidi Brahim' or 'Le Roi s'Amuse';
white gloves and monocles and polished swords

and Dreyfus with his buttons off, chalk-faced
but standing to attention, the school prig
caught in some act and properly disgraced.
A puffy satrap prances on one leg

to snap the traitor's sword, his ordered rage
bursting with 'cran et gloire' and gouts of rouge.
The chargers click and shiver. There is no stir
in the drawn ranks, among the hosts of the air,

all draped and gathered by the weird storm-light
cheap wood-engravings cast on those who fought
at Mars-la-Tour, Sedan; or on the men
in the world-famous stories of Jules Verne

or nailed at Golgotha. Drumrap and fife
hit the right note: 'A mort le Juif! Le Juif
à la lanterne!' Serenely the mob howls,
its silent mouthings hammered into scrolls

torn from *Apocalypse*. No wonder why
we fall to violence out of apathy,
redeemed by falling and restored to grace
beyond the dreams of mystic avarice.

But who are 'we', since history is law,
clad in our skins of silver, steel and hide,
or in our rags, with rotten teeth askew,
heroes or knaves as Clio shall decide?

'We' are crucified Pilate, Caiaphas
in his thin soutane and Judas with the face
of a man who has drunk wormwood. We come
back empty-handed from Jerusalem

counting our blessings, honestly admire
the wrath of the peacemakers, for example
Christ driving the money-changers from the temple,
applaud the Roman steadiness under fire.

We are the occasional just men who sit
in gaunt self-judgment on their self-defeat,
the élite hermits, secret orators
of an old faith devoted to new wars.

We are 'embusqués', having no wounds to show
save from the thorns, ecstatic at such pain.
Once more the truth advances; and again
the metaphors of blood begin to flow.

7

Salute us all, Christus with your iron
garlands of poppies and ripe carrion.
No, sleep where you stand; let some boy-officer
take up your vigil with your dungfork spear.

What vigil is this, then, among the polled
willows, cart-shafts uptilted against skies,
translucent rain at jutting calvaries;
on paths that are rutted and broken-walled?

What is this relic fumbled with such care
by mittened fingers in dugout or bomb-
tattered, jangling estaminet's upper room?
The incense from a treasured tabatière,

you watchmen at the Passion. Péguy said
'why do I write of war? Simply because
I have not been there. In time I shall cease
to invoke it.' We still dutifully read

'heureux ceux qui sont morts'. Drawn on the past
these presences endure; they have not ceased
to act, suffer, crouching into the hail
like labourers of their own memorial

or those who worship at its marble rote,
their many names one name, the common 'dur'
built into duration, the endurance of war;
blind Vigil herself, helpless and obdurate.

And yet what sights: Saul groping in the dust
for his broken glasses, or the men far-gone
on the road to Emmaus who saw the ghost.
Commit all this to memory. The line

falters, reforms, vanishes into the smoke
of its own unknowing; mother, dad,
gone in that shell-burst, with the other dead,
'pour la patrie', according to the book.

8

Dear lords of life, stump-toothed, with ragged breath,
throng after throng cast out upon the earth,
flesh into dust, who slowly come to use
dreams of oblivion in lieu of paradise,

push on, push on! – through struggle, exhaustion,
indignities of all kinds, the impious Christian
oratory, 'vos morituri', through berserk fear,
laughing, howling, 'servitude et grandeur'

in other words, in nameless gobbets thrown
up by the blast, names issuing from mouths
of the dying, with their dying breaths.
But rest assured, bristly-brave gentlemen

of Normandie and Loire. Death does you proud,
every heroic commonplace, 'Amor',
'Fidelitas', polished like old armour,
stamped forever into the featureless mud.

Poilus and sous-officiers who plod
to your lives' end, name your own recompense,
expecting nothing but the grace of France,
drawn to her arms, her august plenitude.

The blaze of death goes out, the mind leaps
for its salvation, is at once extinct;
its last thoughts tetter the furrows, distinct
in dawn twilight, caught on the barbed loops.

Whatever strikes and maims us it is not
fate, to our knowledge. En avant, Péguy!
The irony of advancement. Say 'we
possess nothing; try to hold on to that.'

9

There is an ancient landscape of green branches –
true tempérament de droite, you have your wish –
crosshatching twigs and light, goldfinches
among the peppery lilac, the small fish

pencilled into the stream. Ah, such a land
the Ile de France once was. Virelai and horn
wind through the meadows, the dawn-masses sound
fresh triumphs for our Saviour crowned with scorn.

Good governors and captains, by your leave,
you also were sore-wounded but those wars
are ended. Iron men who bell the hours,
marshals of porte-cochère and carriage-drive,

this is indeed perfection, this is the heart
of the mystère. Yet one would not suppose
Péguy's 'defeat', 'affliction', your lost cause.
Old Bourbons view-hallooing for regret

among the cobwebs and the ghostly wine,
you dream of warrior-poets and the Meuse
flowing so sweetly; the androgynous Muse
your priest-confessor, sister-châtelaine.

How the mood swells to greet the gathering storm!
The chestnut trees begin to thresh and cast
huge canisters of blossom at each gust.
Coup de tonnerre! Bismarck is in the room!

Bad memories, seigneurs? Such wraiths appear
on summer evenings when the gnat-swarm spins
a dying moment on the tremulous air.
The curtains billow and the rain begins

its night-long vigil. Sombre heartwoods gleam,
the clocks replenish the small hours' advance
and not a soul has faltered from its trance.
'Je est un autre', that fatal telegram,

floats past you in the darkness, unreceived.
Connoisseurs of obligation, history
stands, a blank instant, awaiting your reply:
'If we but move a finger France is saved!'

10

Down in the river-garden a grey-gold
dawnlight begins to silhouette the ash.
A rooster wails remotely over the marsh
like Mr Punch mimicking a lost child.

At Villeroy the copybook lines of men
rise up and are erased. Péguy's cropped skull
dribbles its ichor, its poor thimbleful,
a simple lesion of the complex brain.

Woefully battered but not too bloody,
smeared by fraternal root-crops and at one
with the fritillary and the veined stone,
having composed his great work, his small body,

for the last rites of truth, whatever they are,
or the Last Judgment which is much the same,
or Mercy, even, with her tears and fire,
he commends us to nothing, leaves a name

for the burial-detail to gather up
with rank and number, personal effects,
the next-of-kin and a few other facts;
his arm over his face as though in sleep

or to ward off the sun: the body's prayer,
the tribute of his true passion, for Chartres
steadfastly cleaving to the Beauce, for her,
the Virgin of innumerable charities.

'Encore plus douloureux et doux.' Note how
sweetness devours sorrow, renders it again,
turns to affliction each more carnal pain.
Whatever is fulfilled is now the law

where law is grace, that grace won by inches,
inched years. The men of sorrows do their stint,
whose golgothas are the moon's trenches,
the sun's blear flare over the salient.

J'accuse! j'accuse! – making the silver prance
and curvet, and the dust-motes jig to war
across the shaky vistas of old France,
the gilt-edged maps of Strasbourg and the Saar.

Low tragedy, high farce, fight for command,
march, counter-march, and come to the salute
at every hole-and-corner burial-rite
bellowed with hoarse dignity into the wind.

Take that for your example! But still mourn,
being so moved: éloge and elegy
so moving on the scene as if to cry
'in memory of those things these words were born.'

Canaan

That Man as a Rational Animal Desires the Knowledge which is His Perfection

Abiding provenance I would have said
the question stands
                    even in adoration
clause upon clause
                  with or without assent
reason and desire on the same loop –
I imagine singing I imagine

getting it right – the knowledge
of sensuous intelligence
               entering into the work –
spontaneous happiness as it was once
given our sleeping nature to awake by
                        and know
innocence of first inscription

Sobieski's Shield

1

The blackberry, white
field-rose, all others
of that family:

steadfast is the word

and the star-gazing planet out of which
lamentation is spun.

2

Brusque as the year
            purple garish-brown
aster chrysanthemum
            signally restored
to a subsistence of slant light
as one might assert
                        Justice Equity
or Sobieski's Shield even
                        the names
and what they have about them dark to dark.

Of Coming into Being and Passing Away

To Aileen Ireland

Rosa sericea: its red
spurs
      blooded with amber
each lit and holy grain
the sun
      makes much of
as of all our shadows –

prodigal ever returning
darkness that in such circuits
reflects diuturnity
           to itself
and to our selves
           yields nothing
finally –

      but by occasion
visions of truth or dreams
as they arise –
           to terms of grace
where grace has surprised us –
the unsustaining
           wondrously sustained

De Anima

Salutation: it is as though
effortlessly – to reprise –
             the unsung spirit
gestures of no account
become accountable
                such matters arising
whatever it is that is sought

             through metaphysics
research into angelic song
ending as praise itself
the absolute yet again
atoned with the contingent –
             typology
incarnate – Bethlehem the open field –

still to conceive no otherwise: an
aphasia of staring wisdom
the souls images glassily exposed
             fading to silverpoint
still to be at the last
ourselves and masters of all
             humility –

Whether the Virtues are Emotions

Overnight – overnight –
                          the inmost
self made outcast: here
plighting annihilations
                          unfinished
business of eros
                 the common numen

of waking
          reverie where you had dreamt
to be absolved:
                and with the day
forsakenness
             the new bride brought forth:
carnal desuetude

her mystic equity
her natures ripped hardihood
the radiant
            windrows where a storm
emptied its creels
thrusting ailanthus that is called
                 the Tree of Heaven

Whether Moral Virtue Comes by Habituation

It is said that sometimes even fear
drops away –
                  exhausted – I would not
deny that: self
expression – you could argue – the first to go –
immolated
                  selfhood the last:

deprivation therefore
                           dereliction even
become the things we rise to:
ethereal conjecture
                           taking on
humankinds heaviness of purchase
the moral nebulae

                           common as lichen
the entire corpus of ruinous sagesse
moved by some rite
                           and pace of being
as by earth in her slow
                           approaches to withdrawal
the processionals of seared array

Ritornelli

For Hugh Wood on his 60th Birthday

i

Angel of Tones
                flame of accord
exacting mercies
                  answerable
to rage as solace

I will have you sing

ii

For so the judgement
passes
       it is not
otherwise
            hereafter
you will see them resolved
in tears
        they shall bear
your crowns of redress

iii

Lost to no thought
of triumph he returns
upon himself goes down
among water and ash
and wailing sounds confused
with sounds of joy

To William Cobbett: In Absentia

I say it is not faithless
to stand without faith, keeping open
vigil at the site.
Who shall endure? What force throws off
the verdict of each day's
idle and taunting honours,
the lottery, the trade in grief,
the outrageous quittance, the shiftless
orders of fools?
I say let stand the entire
deposed authority
of vision just as it fell;
your righteous unjust and cordial anger,
your singular pitch where labour is spoken of,
your labour that brought to pass
reborn Commodity with uplifted hands
awed by its own predation.

Parentalia

The here-and-now finds vigil transfiguring
whatever is
                    yet ignorant of your beauty.
Any one of us, given a certain light,
                    shall make and be immortal:
streets of Jerusalem, seraphs the passers-by,
and other extras, artisans per diem,
imperative in hindsight
                            a brief blessing.
I cannot tell how we might be otherwise
drawn to the things occluded, manifold,
the measureless that stands
                            even so depleted
in the faint rasp of dry autumnal flowers.

Respublica

The strident high
civic trumpeting
of misrule. It is
what we stand for.

Wild insolence,
aggregates without
distinction. Courage
of common men:

spent in the ruck
their remnant witness
after centuries
is granted them

like a pardon.
And other fealties
other fortitudes
broken as named –

Respublica
brokenly recalled,
its archaic laws
and hymnody;

and destroyed hope
that so many times
is brought with triumph
back from the dead.

De Jure Belli Ac Pacis

i.m. Hans-Bernd von Haeften, 1905–1944

I

The people moves as one spirit unfettered
claim our assessors of stone.
                              When the nations
fall dispossessed such conjurings possess them,
elaborate barren fountains, projected
aqueducts
                    where water is no longer found.
Where would one find Grotius for that matter,
the secular justice clamant among psalms,
huge-fisted visionary Comenius . . .?
Could none predict these haughty degradations
as now your high-strung
                              martyred resistance serves
to consecrate the liberties of Maastricht?

II

*. . . sah er den Erzengel Michael im Kampf gegen den Drachen,
Michael, den Engel der deutschen Geschichte . . .*

The iron-beamed engine-shed has chapel windows.
Glare-eyed, you spun. The hooks are still in the beam;
a sun-patch drains to nothing; here the chocked
blade sluiced into place, here the abused blood
               set its own wreaths.
Time passes, strengthening and fading. Europa
hetaera displays her parts, her triumph
to tax even Dürer's resplendent economy
in rictus and graven sorrow.
                   On some envisioned
rathaus clock, geared like a mill, the dragon
strikes,
       the Archangel, unseeing, unbowed,
chimes with each stroke.

III

You foretold us, hazarding the proscribed tongue
of piety and shame; plain righteousness
committed with much else to Kreisau's bees
for their particular keeping. We might have kept
your Christian inhibitions – faithful, non-jurant,
in the singing-court of dread
                    at the grid of extortion –
but chose pity. This pity is shameless
unlike memory, though both can draw
sugar from iron.
                    Pity, alone with its rage,
settles on multitudes
                    as the phoenix sought
from a hundred cities tribute of requiting flame.

IV

In Plötzensee where you were hanged
                              they now hang
tokens of reparation and in good faith
compound with Cicero's maxims, Schiller's chant,
your silenced verities.
                  To the high-minded
base-metal forgers of this common Europe,
community of parody, you stand ec-
centric as a prophet. There is no better
vision that I can summon: you were upheld
on the strong wings of the Psalms before you died.
Evil is not good's absence but gravity's
everlasting bedrock and its fatal chains
inert, violent, the suffrage of our days.

V

Not harmonies – harmonics, astral whisperings
light-years above the stave; groans, murmurs, cries,
tappings from cell to cell. It is a night-watch,
indeterminate and of vast concentration,
of those redeeming their pledged fear, who strike
faith from the hard rock of God's fallenness;
their pain draws recompense beyond our grasp
of recapitulation.
        Slurred clangour,
cavernous and chained haltings, echo from time's
inchoate music, the theme standing proclaimed
only in the final measures –
                Vexilla regis
uplifted by Rüdiger Schleicher's violin.

VI

der Tod . . . nahm über uns Gewalt,
Hielt uns in seinem Reich gefangen.
Hallelujah!

Those three eternal days Christus did not lie
shackled in death:
                     but found out your stark reich,
deep-buried hypocausts dense for the harrowing,
held there – since time so holds within itself –
slow precise Fellgiebel, chivalrous Hofacker,
clamped in their silence:
                     keeps also Goerdeler's
doubled, many-times-consummated, agony:
in whatever fortress, on whatever foundation,
then, now, in eternum, the spirit bears witness
                     through its broken flesh:
to grace more enduring even than mortal corruption,
ineradicable, and rightly so.

VII

Smart whip-tap at boot-top, absolute
                           licence of the demons
to wreak their correction; elsewhere they are fixed
self-torches in sulphur; as there is a God,
                           elsewhere, of jealous mercy
this is not news: the book of Daniel's strength
unwritten, Zion's resurgent lamentation
in Kreisau's witnessing here undenizened
to the sand, to the old waste.
                           So let the rights
be speculation, fantastic pickings, late
                           gold of Europa
in her brief modish rags –
                           Schindler! Schindler!

VIII

Hinrichtungsstätte war ein Schuppen im Gefängnis . . .

But if – but if; and if nowhere
                        but here
archives for catacombs; letters, codes, prayers,
film-scraps, dossiers, shale of crunched shellac,
new depths of invention, children's
                        songs to mask torture . . .
Christus, it is not your stable: it will serve
as well as any other den or shippen
the arraigned truth, the chorus with its gifts
of humiliation, incense and fumitory,
                        Lucerna,
the soul-flame, as it has stood through such ages,
ebbing, and again, lambent, replenished,
                        in its stoup of clay.

Sorrel

Very common and widely distributed . . . It is called Sorrow . . . in some parts of Worcestershire.

Memory worsening – let it go as rain
streams on half-visible clatter of the wind
     lapsing and rising,
that clouds the pond's green mistletoe of spawn,
seeps among nettlebeds and rust-brown sorrel,
perpetual ivy burrowed by weak light,
makes carved shapes crumble: the ill-weathering stone
salvation's troth-plight, plumed, of the elect.

Parentalia

Daniel 12:3-4, 9

Go your ways, as if in thanksgiving:
Daniel finally instructed of the Lord.
The book is closed for your time; it will not
                    open again to the slow
round of the psalms, the prophets of righteousness.
But go, as instrumental, of the Lord,
                    life-bound to his foreknowledge
and in his absence making your return
to the generations, the rosaceae,
the things of earth snagging the things of grace,
darkened hawthorn, its late flare, that stands
illustrious, and the darkening season –
Harvest Festival to Armistice Day
                    the other harvest.

Mysticism and Democracy

I am of Dark-land, for there I was born, and there my
Father and Mother are still.

To the Evangelicals: a moving image
of multitudes turned aside –
                              into the fields –
with staves and bundles, through the patched sloughs,
broken-down hedges, among brick stacks:
unerring the voice, the direction, though the truth
                              is difficult to follow,
a track of peculiar virtue – English – which so often
                              deceives us by the way.
Exhaustion is of the essence, though in the meantime
what song has befallen those who were laggard
pilgrims, or none. It is as you see. I would not
trouble greatly to proclaim this.
                    But shelve it under Mercies.

Churchill's Funeral

I

. . . one dark day in the Guildhall: looking at the memorials of the city's great past & knowing well the history of its unending charity, I seemed to hear far away in the dim roof a theme, an echo of some noble melody . . .

Endless London
mourns for that knowledge
under the dim roofs
of smoke-stained glass,

the men hefting
their accoutrements
of webbed tin, many
in bandages,

with cigarettes,
with scuffed hands aflare,
as though exhaustion
drew them to life;

as if by some
miraculous draft
of enforced journeys
their peace were made

strange homecoming
into sleep, blighties,
and untouched people
among the maimed:

nobilmente it
rises from silence,
the grand tune, and goes
something like this.

II

*Suppose the subject of inquiry, instead of being House-law (Oikonomia),
had been star-law (Astronomia), and that, ignoring distinction between
stars fixed and wandering, as here between wealth radiant and wealth
reflective, the writer had begun thus:*

Innocent soul
ghosting for its lost
twin, the afflicted one,
born law-giver;

uncanny wraith
kindled afar-off
like the evening star,
res publica

seen by itself
with its whole shining
history discerned
through shining air,

both origin
and consequence, its
hierarchies of sorts,
fierce tea-making

in time of war,
courage and kindness
as the marvel is
the common weal

that will always,
simply as of right,
keep faith, ignorant
of right or fear:

who is to judge
who can judge of this?
Maestros of the world
not you not them.

III

Los listens to the Cry of the Poor Man; his Cloud
Over London in volume terrific low bended in anger.

The copper clouds
are not of this light;
Lambeth is no more
the house of the lamb.

The meek shall die rich
would you believe:
with such poverty
lavished upon them,

with their obsequies
the Heinkels' lourd drone
and Fame darkening
her theatres

to sirens, laughter,
the frizzed angels
of visitation
powdered by the blast,

the catafalques
like gin-palaces
where she entertains
the comedians.

IV

St Mary Abchurch, St Mary Aldermanbury, St Mary-le-Bow . . .

Stone Pietà
for which the city
offers up incense
and ashes, blitzed

firecrews, martyrs
crying to the Lord,
their mangled voices
within the flame;

to which we bring
litanies of scant
survival and all
random mercies,

with the ragwort
and the willow-herb
as edifiers
of ruined things.

V

. . . every minute particular, the jewels of Albion, running down
The kennels of the streets & lanes as if they were abhorr'd.

The brazed city
reorders its own
destruction, admits
the strutting lords

to the temple,
vandals of sprayed blood –
obliterations
to make their mark.

The spouting head
spiked as prophetic
is ancient news.
Once more the keeper

of the dung-gate
tells his own story;
so too the harlot
of many tears.

Speak now regardless
judges of the hour:
what verdict, what people?
Hem of whose garment?

Whose Jerusalem –
at usance for its bones'
redemption and last
salvo of poppies?

Pisgah

I am ashamed and grieve, having seen you then,
those many times, as now
                              you turn to speak
with someone standing deeper in the shade;
or fork a row, or pace to the top end
where the steep garden overlooks the house;
around you the cane loggias, tent-poles, trellises,
the flitter of sweet peas caught in their strings,
the scarlet runners, blossom that seems to burn
an incandescent aura towards evening.
This half-puzzled, awkward surprise is yours;
you cannot hear me or quite make me out.
Formalities preserve us:
                              perhaps I too am a shade.

Mysticism and Democracy

i

Ill-conceived, ill-ordained, heart's rhetoric:
hour into hour the iron nib hardly
                                pausing at the well –
inscribed silver, facets of Stourbridge glass,
polished desk surface; the darkling mirrors
                        to an occult terrain:
mystical democracy, ill-gotten, ill-bestowed,
as if, long since, we had cheated them,
                                our rightful, righteous
masters, as though they would pay us back
                                terrific freedoms –
Severn at the flood, streaked pools that are called
                                                flashes
wind-beaten to a louring shine.

ii

Let this not fall imputed to our native
                                obdurate credulities.
Contrariwise within its own doctrine it spins,
remote saturnian orb: oblivious
the imperial granites, braided, bunched, and wreathed;
                                the gilded ornature
ennobling lowly errors – exacted, from exalted –
                                tortuous in their simplicity;
the last unblemished records of service
                                                left hanging
in air yellowed with a late half-light
as votive depositions
                        not to be taken down.

from *Psalms of Assize*

I

Hinc vagantur in tenebris misere, quia non credunt veritati ipsi . . .
Querunt lumen confisi ipsis et non inveniunt.

Why should I strike you with my name
why trade impress of proud wounds
come now belated
                                    patrons of wrath
anxieties are not rectitudes
holiness itself falls
to unholy rejoicing
to resurrect the dead
myth
            of our salvation
blasphemies no less
mercies
                let us pray
Gabriel descend
as a mood almost
                            a monody
of chloroform
or florists roses
consensual angel spinning his words
                                    thread
he descends
                        and light
sensitive darkness
                                    follows him down

II

Non potest quisquam utrisque servire, simulque ascendere et descendere; aut ascendas aut descendas oportet . . .

Ascend through declension
the mass the matter
the gross refinement
   gravitas
everlasting obsession
vanity by grace
the starred
         misattributed
works of survival
attributes even now
hallowing consequence
chants of the trace elements
the Elohim
         unearthly music
given to the world
message what message
         doubtless
the Lord knows
when he will find us
       if ever
we shall see him
with the elect
        justified
   to his right hand

IV

*Hac sola ratione semper eris liber: si volueris
quaecuumque fiunt ita fieri, et omnia in
bonam partem verte.*

Seeing how they stand
with what odds
                by what rule
of accidence resolved
the irresolute
                the feats
of hapless jubilo
                the gifts
set down to derision
rejoice in them
as things that are mourned
loving kindness
                and mercy
righteousness
patient abiding
and whatever good
is held
        untenable
the entire complex dance
of simple atonement
as in a far fetched
                comedy
making of sleep and time
timeless healers

VII

Victo carne et sanguine restant demones;
numquam vitabimus. Huc illuc semper adest.

The great O of advent
    cum sibylla
O that nothing may touch
this unapproachable
levity of the creator
conscience and guilt
the formal alchemy
not held to trial
for what is beyond
such mercurial reckoning
its ultimate
        cadence
its fall impeccable
the condign
        salvation
pure carnival in the spirit
        even so
God of miracles the crying
        even so
this is how it ends
how it goes at the last day
        spargens sonum
the day of bitten tongues
say what you like

Of Constancy and Measure

i.m. Ivor Gurney

One sees again how it goes:
rubble ploughed in and salted
                              the bloods
haphazard fatalities
our scattering selves allowed
their glimpse of restitution –
                              the orchards
of Sarras or Severn bare
plenitude first and last –
as if constancy were in time
given its own for keeping
                              as such gifts belong
to the unfailing burden of the planet
with so much else believed to be fire and air

To the High Court of Parliament

November 1994

– who could outbalance poised
                    Marvell; balk the strength
of Gillray's unrelenting, unreconciling mind;
grandees risen from scavenge; to whom Milton
                    addressed his ideal censure:
once more, singular, ill-attended,
staid and bitter Commedia – as she is called –
delivers to your mirth her veiled presence.

None the less amazing: Barry's and Pugin's grand
dark-lantern above the incumbent Thames.
You: as by custom unillumined
                    masters of servile counsel.
Who can now speak for despoiled merit,
                    the fouled catchments of Demos,
as 'thy' high lamp presides with sovereign
equity, over against us, across this
densely reflective, long-drawn, procession of waters?

The Triumph of Love

I

Sun-blazed, over Romsley, a livid rain-scarp.

II

Guilts were incurred in that place, now I am convinced:
self-molestation of the child-soul, would that be it?

III

Petronius Arbiter, take us in charge;
carry us with you to the house of correction.
Angelus Silesius, guard us while we are there.

IV

Ever more protracted foreplay,
never ending – *o ewigkeit* – no act
the act of oblivion, the blown
aorta pelting out blood.

V

Obstinate old man – *senex
sapiens*, it is not. What is he saying;
why is he still so angry? He says, I cannot
forgive myself. We are immortal.
Where was I? Prick him.

VI

Between bay window and hedge the impenetrable holly
strikes up again taut wintry vibrations.
The hellebore is there still,
half-buried; the crocuses are surviving.

From the front room I might be able to see
the coal fire's image planted in a circle
of cut-back rose bushes. Nothing is changed
by the strength of this reflection.

VII

Romsley, of all places! – Spraddled ridge-
village sacred to the boy-martyr,
Kenelm, his mouth full of blood and toffee.
A stocky water tower built like the stump
of a super-dreadnought's foremast. It could have set
Coventry ablaze with pretend
broadsides, some years before that armoured
city suddenly went down, guns
firing, beneath the horizon; huge silent whumphs
of flame-shadow bronzing the nocturnal
cloud-base of her now legendary dust.

IX

On chance occasions –
and others have observed this – you can see the wind,
as it moves, barely a separate thing,
the inner wall, the cell, of an hourglass, humming
vortices, bright particles in dissolution,
a roiling plug of sand picked up
as a small dancing funnel. It is how
the purest apprehension might appear
to take corporeal shape.

X

Last things first; the slow haul to forgive them:
Chamberlain's compliant vanity, his pawn ticket saved
from the antepenultimate ultimatum; their strict

pudency, but not to national honour; callous
discretion; their inwardness with things of the world;
their hearing as a profound music
the hollow lion-roar of the slammed vaults;
the decent burials at the eleventh hour:
their Authorized Version – it has seen better days –
'nation shall not lift up sword against nation'
or 'nation shall rise up against nation' (a later
much-revised draft of the treaty). In either case
a telling figure out of rhetoric,
epanalepsis, the same word first and last.

XI

Above Dunkirk, the sheared anvil-
head of the oil-smoke column, the wind
beginning to turn, turning on itself, spiralling,
shaped on its potter's wheel. But no fire-storm:
such phenomena were as yet unvisited
upon Judeo-Christian-Senecan Europe.
It is to *Daniel*, as to our own
tragic satire, that one returns
for mastery of the business; well-timed,
intermitted terror. How else recall
Mierendorff's ancient, instant, final cry –
madness – in Leipzig, out of the sevenfold
fiery furnace?

XIII

Whose lives are hidden in God? Whose?
Who can now tell what was taken, or where,
or how, or whether it was received:
how ditched, divested, clamped, sifted, over-
laid, raked over, grassed over, spread around,
rotted down with leafmould, accepted

as civic concrete, reinforceable
base cinderblocks:
tipped into Danube, Rhine, Vistula, dredged up
with the Baltic and the Pontic sludge:
committed *in absentia* to solemn elevation,
Trauermusik, musique funèbre, funeral
music, for male and female
voices ringingly *a cappella*,
made for double string choirs, congregated brass,
choice performers on baroque trumpets hefting,
like glassblowers, inventions
of supreme order?

XIX

If you so wish to construe this, I shall say
only: the Jew is not beholden
to forgiveness, of pity. You will have to
go forward block by block, for pity's sake,
irresolute as granite. Now
move to the next section.

XX

From the *Book of Daniel*, am I correct?
Quite correct, sir. Permit me:
refocus that Jew – yes there,
that one. You see him burning,
dropping feet first, in a composed manner,
still in suspension,
from the housetop.
It will take him for ever
caught at this instant
of world-exposure.
In close-up he maintains appearance –
Semitic ur-Engel –

terminal agony none the less
interminable, the young
martyrs ageing in the fire –
thank you, Hauptmann – Schauspieler? –
Run it through again and for ever
he stretches his wings of flame
upon instruction.

XXIV

Summon the leaders, the leaping captions,
numbers rolled from a drum: Cardanus
on the significance of eclipses,
Rathenau, 'industrialist and philosopher',
famous unnamed assassins' open tourers,
a road slicked in its dressing of lime pollen.
After some early clouds burn off
as predicted by the harbour master
we will have a clear day –
lake water chopping under paddle-boxes,
the scroll-wave motion of a carrousel,
jelly-green celluloid eye-shields; children
overexcited by rampageous clowns,
fire-breathers, artists of inept escape.

XXV

The hierarchies are here to be questioned. Lead on
Angelus Novus; show onetime experts presenting
aniline dyes as the intensest expressions
of coal-tar; let others develop 'man's
determinate action', for so Peirce dubbed it
in the wake of Chickamauga. Failing these,
bring others well-tried in the practical
worlds of illusion, builders of fabled masks,
their dancing clients

vanishing into the work
made up as lords and spiky blackamoors:
Unveil the dust-wrapped, post-war architects'
immediate prize-designs in balsa wood,
excelling fantasies, sparsely inhabited
by spaced-out, pinhead model citizens:
Florentine piazzas for Antarctica.
The augurs, finally: strangely possessed by doubt
whether to address the saturnine magistrates
concerning the asteroid, or the asteroid
on the nature of destiny and calculation.

XXVIII

As I have at times imagined: Melancholy,
the more inert we are, thrusts us
into the way of things violently
uprooted. And there, for her own
increase, grants us a little possession,
that we may then lose all. *Boerenverdriet* –
peasant sorrow? peasant affliction? – you cannot
cease feeling their uncouth terror, whose flesh
is our own. The slaughterers relish this work
of sport: *landsknechts* as Callot depicts them,
hideously-festive-death's foragers;
so he draws them among us,
slouch-feathered, shin-booted, jangle
of sloven-worn iron: *ruyter, ritterkind,*
rutterkin, over the low shrub hill – hoyda!
hoyda! – heel-kicking their nags.

XXIX

What is this strange tree that bears so well
such heavy fruit commingled with new blossom;
and who are these

hanging amid the branches,
in bonds of remonstrance,
like traitors like martyrs?
This is our Upas tree; it is a tree of sleep
that never breaks; it is our politic
transcendent shade.
It is England's
iron-bound storm-tree turbulently at rest.

XXXVIII

Widely established yet with particular
local intensities, the snow
half-thawed now hardens over again,
glassen-ridged, or pashed
like fish-ice: refracted light
red against copper. The hedged sun
draws into itself for its self-quenching.
If one is so minded, these modalities
stoop to re-enter the subterrane of faith –
faith, that is, in real Being;
the real being God or, more comprehensively, Christ –
as a sanctuary lamp treadles its low flame
or as the long-exiled *Salve Regina* was sung
in the crypt at Lastingham on the threshold
of a millennium.

XLIV

Cry pax. Not that anything is forgiven;
not that there seems anything new to forgive
in this assemblance. Not that the assemblance
might be tempted into the fertile
wilderness of unspirituality. Not that I
know the way out, or in. So be it;

let us continue to abuse one another
with the kiss of peace.

XLV

It is believed – argued – they offered him
some kind of painkiller, which
is plausible. In any event
he would not touch it.
Morus, humble and witty at the end,
glad of a clean death;
Southwell, addressing the cordial
cordially: 'it does my heart good'.
Fifty years without limbs, or in an iron
lung, is that possible? I lose
courage but courage is not lost.

XLVII

Movie-vocals cracked, her patter still
bright as the basement gents' brass taps at the Town Hall.
Benevolent, like a Young Fabians' Club
vision of labour; invariable routine
produced the same hot water, brought to the boil
her honest yodelling. So she fetched home the lads
from France, as once she had marched the lasses back
to a silent mill. She, and her armed
aspidistra, last off the beaches.

L

Trimalchio, bouncing up from a brief seventh
bout of financial ruin, pledges us
his high-spent poverty with distasteful feast.
He is himself already, so he claims,
in his seventh element.

He merits, I would say, a loaded rumour
among the legends that now circulate
about Canary Wharf, the Isle of Dogs,
new comets whiffling in and out of orbit.
Time's satire, for its part, allows his status
not worse than that clay-footed emperor –
barely saluted at his last ascension – flung
arse-over-tip to belching Tartarus,
with coarsest imputations, by the gods:
roof-crashing his own dull funeral-orgy,
the never-finished ritual deification,
making a clown-shaped hole in the sacred floor.
Trimalchio readjusts his mask of laughter.

LI

Whatever may be meant by *moral landscape*,
it is for me increasingly a terrain
seen in cross-section: igneous, sedimentary,
conglomerate, metamorphic rock-
strata, in which particular grace,
individual love, decency, endurance,
are traceable across the faults.

LII

Admittedly at times this moral landscape
to my exasperated ear emits
archaic burrings like a small, high-fenced
electricity sub-station of uncertain age
in a field corner where the flies
gather and old horses shake their sides.

LIII

But leave it now, leave it; as you left
a washed-out day at Stourport or the Lickey,
improvised rainhats mulch for papier-mâché,
and the chips floating.
Leave it now, leave it; give it over
to that all-gathering general English light,
in which each separate bead
of drizzle at its own thorn-tip stands
as revelation.

LIV

Entertainment overkill: that amplifier
acts as the brain of the putsch. The old
elixir-salesmen had no such entourage
though their product was superior; as was
their cunning oratory.
For the essentials of the cadre, Wordsworth's
'savage torpor' can hardly be bettered
or his prescience refuted.
What it is they possess – and, at some mean
level, Europe lies naked to their abuse –
is not immediately
in the grasp of their hand. They are vassal-
lord-puppet-strutters, not great scourges of God.
A simple text would strike them
dumb, and is awaited. Meanwhile
they are undeniable powers of this world,
closely attended in their performance
of sacral baseness, like kings at stool.

LV

Vergine bella – it is here that I require
a canzone of some substance. There are sound
precedents for this, of a plain eloquence
which would be perfect. But –
ought one to say, I am required; or, it is
required of me; or, it is requisite that I should
make such an offering, bring in such a tribute?
And is this real obligation or actual
pressure of expectancy? One cannot purchase
the goodwill of your arduously simple faith
as one would acquire a tobacconist's cum paper shop
or a small convenience store
established by aloof, hardworking Muslims.
Nor is language, now, what it once was
even in – wait a tick – nineteen hundred and forty-
five of the common era, when your blast-scarred face
appeared staring, seemingly in disbelief,
shocked beyond recollection, unable to recognize
the mighty and the tender salutations
that slowly, with innumerable false starts, the ages
had put together for your glory
in words and in the harmonies of stone.
But you have long known and endured all things
since you first suffered the Incarnation:
endless the extortions, endless the dragging
in of your name. *Vergine bella*, as you
are well aware, I here follow
Petrarch, who was your follower,
a sinner devoted to your service.
I ask that you acknowledge the work
as being contributive to your high praise,
even if no-one else shall be reconciled
to a final understanding of it in that light.

LVIII

Portrait of mourning's autodidact: proud,
not willing to drop the increasingly
evident burden of shamed
gratitude: to his own dead,
and to those not his own – Pandora
Barraclough, for instance;
his desire to keep alive
recollection of what they were put to, though
not for his sake, not for this future, and not
'rooted', God help us; they were as he
now is; dispossessed
even in the scant subsistence
of disturbed folk-memory. Each time,
the salving of the waste
less and less expected;
yet time and again salvific –
like the barely recognized
beauty of the potato vine in its places
of lowly flowering.

LXIX

What choice do you have? These are false questions.
Fear is your absolute, yet in each feature
infinitely variable, Manichean beyond dispute,
for you alone, the skeletal maple, a loose wire
tapping the wind.

LXXI

If slab faces can be wolfish this appears
in the tall glare of sodium light on snow.
Fairground-mirror distortion kneads us all
stocking-masks. I have not forgotten

crowd-demonry, the pulley-grins of the Flemish
tormentors. Should I subpoena Callot's
and Goya's witness to that which is in
[read: of] the natural archetype? It is the sheer
descent, the acceleration, that for us
now is terrible: unselfbeing – each held
distracted in the doomed body-cockpit
by a velocity which is also inertia,
round-the-clock idle talk-down to impact.

LXXVI

At seven, even, I knew the much-vaunted
Battle was a dud. First it was a dud,
then a gallant write-off. Honour the young men
whose eager fate was to steer that droopy *coque*
against the Meuse bridgeheads. The Fairey
Swordfish had an ungainly frail strength,
cranking in at sea level, wheels whacked
by Channel spindrift. Ingratitude
still gets to me, the unfairness
and waste of survival; a nation
with so many memorials but no memory.

LXXVII

By what right did Keyes, or my cousin's
Lancaster, or the trapped below-decks watch
of Peter's clangorous old destroyer-escort,
serve to enfranchise these strange children
pitiless in their ignorance and contempt?
I know places where grief has stood mute-
howling for half a century, self
grafted to unself till it is something like
these now-familiar alien hatreds,
coarse efflorescence over the dead

proprieties; strong words of Christian hope,
sub rosa, the unmentionable graffiti.

XCI

Celebrate yet again the mind's eye's
dreadful kink or reach of resurrection –
the British walking-wounded – these are like
bunched final stragglers in a three-legged
marathon – last-gasp survivors, loud roll-calls
of the mute orphans, child-victims
in mill and mine. Here's your Lost Empire
Medal for a life spent giving blood. Not
celebrate. Calibrate. Seniors
to synchronize watches. Last rum and fireworks.

XCVII

Devouring our names they possess and destroy
by numbers: the numbered, the numberless
as graphs of totality pose annihilation.
Each sensate corpse, in its fatal
mass-solitariness, excites
multiples of infliction. A particular
dull yard on a dull, smoky day. This, and this,
the unique face, indistinguishable, this, these,
choked in a cess-pit of leaking Sheol.

CI

Though already too late we must
set out early, taking the cinder
path by the old scythe-works. There will be
no quarrel between us – all this time –
a light rain unceasing, the moist woods
full of wild garlic.

CXIV

From the Angels of Irrational
Decision and of Reversed Order
to the Angel of Improvisation:
from the Angel of Improvisation
to the Angels of Tannic
Acid, Salicyl, and Plain Water:
from the Angel of Advantage – where is
the Angel of Recorded Delivery? –
from the Angels of Advantage
Lost, of Sacrifice, of Surrender,
to the Angels of Merciful
Intervention and Final Custody.

CXVII

A noble vernacular? We could screw him,
finish him, for all that. Then he ought
to be happy: a reborn ageing child,
privileged to no place of honour, sated
with dissatisfactions; his wardrobe
of curial cast-offs,
student of Livy in his father's house,
his father being the bailiff – three pounds
a week, rent-free. But all that *unheimlich*
work of his: salutes and cenotaphs,
and vessels moving seaward, the ebb tide
purled in their wake. We cannot
have some great instauration occurring
by default, can we?

CXX

As with the Gospels, which it is allowed to resemble,
in *Measure for Measure* moral uplift

is not the issue. Scrupulosity, diffidence,
shrill spirituality, conviction, free expression,
come off as poorly as deceit or lust.
The ethical *motiv* is – so we may hazard –
opportunism, redemptive and redeemed;
case-hardened on case-law, casuistry's
own redemption; the general temper
a caustic equity.

CXXI

So what is faith if it is not
inescapable endurance? Unrevisited, the ferns
are breast-high, head-high, the days
lustrous, with their hinterlands of thunder.
Light is this instant, far-seeing
into itself, its own
signature on things that recognize
salvation. I
am an old man, a child, the horizon
is Traherne's country.

CXXVI

To the short-sighted Citizen
Angel, the Angel of Assimilation –
'I will not run, dance, kow-tow, to entertain
thugs, perverts, parvenus, perjurers' –
from the stifled Lamentation Angel.
To that dying power from the trim,
well-clad Angel of Death: his insignia
and instruments ——————
From that, to the violated Angel
of Eternal Audit. And to eternity
the ashen-fleshed, wrenched-silent,
untouched, unhearing, Angel of Forgiveness.

CXXVII

In loco parentis – devoured
by mad dad. Hideous – hideous – and many like it –

CXXVIII

The rough-edged, increasingly concave,
line of advance
stops dead: machine-guns do the work
of trick photography. The next trick also
requires apparatus: a sector
chitters brave tries at synchronized push-ups;
by magic the order stands – to remain – pitched
slightly forward against unseen resistance.
Cocteau *flânéed* the First War. After the Second
he moved angles, elevations, to revitalize
young gay men mercurial whom he lifted
out of the tribunals, fabled interrogations,
the cellars, of his fantastical *milice*.
Dipping their (rubber-sheathed) hands to the wrist
in vats of quicksilver, they were absorbed
by bedroom-mirrors through which the interchange
of life with death began and ended. It
is hard now to recover how his debellated,
debellished land bore to inaugurate
towers of remembrance, the massive
verticals, to lean on fields of the dead;
the fields of preservation, with ranging
shadows cast by the black bulk
of light, that are formal sorrow, mourning,
in its conjurations of triumphs.

CXXXVII

The glowering carnival: nightly solar-flare
from the Black Country; minatory beacons
of ironstone, sulphur. Then, greying, east-northeast,
Lawrence's wasted pit-villages rising early,
spinning-wheel gear-iron girding above each
iron garth; old stanchions wet with field-dew.

CXLI

From the terrible Angel of Procreation
to the Angel-in-hiding of Senility.
To the Autonomous Angel
from the several Angels of Solitude:
cc Angel of Self-Alienation,
Angel of Solitary Confinement.
From the Angel of the Morning Gold-fix
to the Angels of Mandragora and Rip-off.
To the Demotic Angels from the Angels
of Repulsion-Attraction, the loud-
winged Angels of Equal Sacrifice, the sole
Angel standing in for Hope and Despair.

CXLII

To the Angel of the Approved Estimates,
to the Angels of Promise Across the Entire
Spectrum. To the Surplus Angels of Acquisition.
I cannot even hear the new instructions,
let alone obey them. Where,
you will say, does explanation
end and confession begin? To know all
is to forgive all: a maxim more wicked,
even, than it is stupid – forgive me,
would you, ever? – But that, by my reckoning,

is not the sum. I have introduced,
it is true, *Laus et vituperatio*
as a formality; still this formal thing
is less clear *in situ*. That –
possibly – is why I appeal to it. The Angels
of Sacral Equivocation, they now tell me,
are redundant: we have lost the *Bloody Question*
[*vide* State Trials (Elizabethan) – ED].
Though you can count on there being some
bloody question or other, one does more
than barely survive. Less hangs on the outcome,
or by, or around, it. Why do I think –
urgently – of beach-sewage? At one source,
Moltke, the two Bonhoeffers, von Haeften,
suffered the Bloody Question and did
nobly thereby. Late praise costs nothing.
To the Angels of Inconclusive Right
on Both Sides, to the Angel of the Last
Minutes, to the Angel of Our
Estimated Times of Arrival and Departure.

CXLIII

Power and sycophancy, sycophancy in power:
power's own cringing to extrapolation
and false prophecy. Subways of white tile
smeared with obscene brown banners. Foucault
running there for his life. Synaesthesia
of appeasement's brain-stench.

CXLVI

The whole-keeping of Augustine's City of God
is our witness; vindicated – even to us –
in a widow's portion of the Law's
majesty of surrender. A hundred

words – or fewer – engrafted by Tyndale's
unshowy diligence: it is all there
but we are not all there, read that how you will.
Cursed be he that removeth his neighbour's mark:
Mosaic statute, to which Ruskin was steadfast.
(If Pound had stood so, he would not have foundered.)
Paul's reinscription of the Kenotic Hymn –
God . . . made himself of no reputation . . . took
the shape of a servant – is our manumission,
Zion new-centred at the circumference
of the world's concentration. Ruskin's wedded
incapacity, for which he has been scourged
many times with derision, does not
render his vision blind or his suffering
impotent. Fellow-labouring master-
servant of *Fors Clavigera*, to us he appears
some half-fabulous field-ditcher who prised
up, from a stone-wedged hedge-root, the lost
amazing crown.

CXLVIII

Obnoxious means, far back within itself,
easily wounded. But vulnerable, proud
anger is, I find, a related self
of covetousness. I came late
to seeing that. Actually, I had to be
shown it. What I saw was rough, and still
pains me. Perhaps it should pain me more.
Pride is our crux: be angry, but not proud
where that means vainglorious. Take Leopardi's
words or – to be accurate – BV's English
cast of them: when he found Tasso's poor
scratch of a memorial barely showing
among the cold slabs of defunct pomp. It
seemed *a sad and angry consolation.*

So – Croker, MacSikker, O'Shem – I ask you:
what are poems for? They are to console us
with their own gift, which is like perfect pitch.
Let us commit that to our dust. What
ought a poem to be? Answer, *a sad
and angry consolation*. What is
the poem? What figures? Say,
a sad and angry consolation. That's
beautiful. Once more? *A sad and angry
consolation*.

CXLIX

Obstinate old man – *senex
sapiens*, it is not. Is he still
writing? What is he writing now? He
has just written: I find it hard
to forgive myself. We are immortal. Where
was I? –

CL

Sun-blazed, over Romsley, the livid rain-scarp.

Speech! Speech!

1

Erudition. Pain, Light. Imagine it great
unavoidable work; although: heroic
verse a non-starter, says PEOPLE. Some believe
we over-employ our gifts. Given identical
street parties, confusion, rapid exposure,
practise self-emulation: music for crossed
hands; for two fingers; music
for taxiing to take-off; for cremation.
Archaic means ∣ files pillaged and erased
in one generation. Judge the distance.
Innocent bystanders on stand-by. Painful
scenes mar final auto-da-fé.

3

How is it tuned, how can it be untuned,
with lithium, this harp of nerves? Fare well
my daimon, inconstant
measures, mood- and mind-stress, heart's rhythm
suspensive; earth-stalled ∣ the wings of suspension.
To persist without sureties ∣ take
any accommodation. What if Scattergood
Commodity took all? Very well ∣ you
shall have on demand, by return, *presto*,
my contractual retraction.
Laser it off the barcode or simply
cut here –

6

They invested – were invested – in proprieties,
where cost can outweigh reward. Decency, duty,
fell through the floorboards (*applause*). I cannot
do more now than gape or grin

haplessly. On self-advisement I erased
WE, though I | is a shade too painful, even
among these figures tying confession
to parody (*laughter*). But surely that's
not all? Rorke's Drift, the great-furnaced
ships off Jutland? They have their own
grandeur, those formal impromptus played
on instruments of the period (*speech! speech!*).

10

From the beginning the question how to end
has been part of the act. One cannot have sex
fantasies (any way) as the final
answer to life. Shiftless,
we are working at it, butt-headed
Sothsegger for one, between bouts of sleep
and community arm-wrestling, elbows
in spilt beer. TALK ABOUT LAUGH, TALK ABOUT
ANGRY. But don't count, don't bet,
on who or what ends uppermost, the franchise
of slavishness being free to all comers
without distinction.

11

Is MUST a true imperative of OUGHT? Is it
that which impels? In the small hours a red
biro clown-paints my pyjamas. Mirrors
disclose no exit-wound. Scrupulosity
unnerved so | *gelassenheit* is a becoming
right order, heart's ease, a gift in faith,
most difficult among freedoms. That's
fair enough, given injustice. Each strafe
throws in some duds, freak chances. The libido
of eunuchs, they say, is terrible. God

how I'd like to, if I could only,
shuffle off alive.

15

About time and about this time ˡ when all
her days are fulfilled: as at Pentecost
or at the Nativity, the Godhead
with her in spirit, like a flint arrow-head
touched to a vapour, a flame. *Intacta*,
through many roads despoiled. The bride of tongues
intimately perfect, perfect though untimely;
not our day. Believe it ˡ Augustine
saved himself for this: the City of God
riding her storm-sewers, towering
at watch and ward, prophetic, exposed
to obscurity, hidden in revelation.

16

First day of the first week: rain
on perennial ground cover, a sheen
like oil of verdure where the rock shows through;
dark ochre patched more dark, with stubborn glaze;
rough soggy drystone clinging to the fell,
broken by hawthorns. What survives
of memory ˡ you can call indigenous
if you recall anything. Finally
untranscribable, that which is ˡ wrests back
more than can be revived; inuring us
through deprivation ˡ below and beyond life,
hard-come-by loss of self ˡ self's restitution.

THEY tell you that? Spiritual osmosis
mystique of argot – I like the gestures
that come with it: a kind of dumb thieves' cant.
SPI−RI−TU−ALI−TY | I salute you
Ich kann nicht anders. It was not so much
cultic pathology I had in mind
as ethical satire; but you wriggle so,
old shape-shifter. Since I am compromised
I shall say more. Assume the earphones. Not
music. Hebrew. Poetry aspires
to the condition of Hebrew. Say that it ís
a wind in the mulberry trees: who will know?

22

Age of mass consent: go global with her.
Challenge satellite failure, the primal
violent day-star moody as Herod.
Forget nothing. Reprieve no-one. Exempt
only her bloodline's *jus natalium.*
Pledge to immoderacy the outraged
hardly forgiven mourning of the PEOPLE,
inexorable, though in compliance,
media-conjured. Inscrutable Í call
her spirit nów on this island: memory
subsiding into darkness | nowhere
coming to rest.

24

Diminishment | the long-withheld secret
of dying. The mind's threatened attention spared
by what it gives up; as by these dark
roses in rain-bleached tubs. Things to be taken

further | let me confess. Strategies
are not salvation: fár fróm it. Even so
REDUCE means LEAD BACK (into the right way),
mortal self-recognition. Patience
is hard, reductive. What comes next?
What shall I say: we múst be animal
to some purpose? My God, who else heard UNHINGE
YOUR JAW, DO IT LIKE A PYTHON | and díd she?

26

No time at all really | a thousand years.
When are computers peerless, folk
festivals not health hazards? Why and how
in these orations do I twist my text?
APPLY FOR FAST RELIEF. Dystopia
on Internet: profiles of the new age;
great gifts unprized; craven audacity's
shockers; glow-in-the-dark geriatric
wigs from old candy-floss (*cat-calls, cheers*).
Starved fourteenth-century mystics write of LOVE.
When in doubt perform. Stick to the much-used
CHECKMATE condom (*laughter, cries of 'shame'*).

34

That caught-short trot-pace of early film: did minds
adjust automatically then? Coúld they
watch the stiff gallantry jig-jog, go knees up
into, half-over, the wire | follow it and know
this was nót farce – whatever else in thát line
might get them howling, have them dress ranks
to Chaplin's forwards-backwards fame and luck?
Such formalities! Thís after a rare
projection of WINGS: heroic lip-readers
in action – one last sortie and – bingo! –

ventriloquists on sight, choked mouthings PER
ARDUA, the eloquent belly-blood.

35

Say you dispute the audit – no offence
to her intended (or to her intended) –
pending the hierarchies so soon to be
remade ǀ though not with her demotic splendour.
Fantastic, apocryphal, near fatalistic
love of one's country ǀ bearing wíth it
always something under-or over-subscribed,
bound to its modicum of the outrageous,
cartoon-animation: jovial, martial,
charwomen, their armour bristles and pails,
dancing – marching – in and out of time –
to Holst's JUPITER ǀ ás to JERUSALEM.

36

Huntress? No not thát huntress but some
other creature of fable. And then for her ǀ
like being hunted. Or inescapably
beholden (this should sound tired but not
emotional to excess). Half forgotten
in one lifetime the funeral sentences
instantly resurrected – hów can they do it?
Whatever of our loves here lies apart:
Whatever it is ǀ you look for in sleep:
simple bio-degradation, a slather
of half-rotted black willow leaves
at the lake's edge.

37

These I imagine are the humble homes
the egalitarian anti-élitist SUN
condescends to daily. Democracy
is in the voice – Churchill's or some other –
I cannot now hear; and the missing clue
WANHOPE: missing, that is, from the game
celebrity plays us for; not lost, since I
still seem to possess it. You too, Jack! –
know who I mean, eh? – poet and scholar
caught sashaying your shadow self. Say that
at normal walking speed, toes on the line.
Say: SURE SUCCESS OF RAP PAR FOR THE COURSE.

38

Do nothing but assume the PEOPLE's voice,
its speaking looks of dumb insolence.
Xenophobic still ǀ the Brits are heroes
living as they have to – short-cuts, thwartings,
one circus act after another, the Powers
enlightened, vengeful: no darkness more
difficult of encounter. Show the folks
Caravaggio's FLAGELLATION – what's it worth? –
sensational, unfeeling. Award
damages for and against the press.
Why is the wreck still singing? All at once
to speak well of thís – A FINE STORY!

44

It now seems probable that I have had
a vision or seizure – some stroke of luck
(see thirty-nine, *supra*). HE'S GOT A NERVE!
Cross-hatch the basilisk behind bars.

Cryptic third-degree: is the dandelion
alone parthenogenic, strange virgin tribe
of scorched earth? STOP WRITING. HANDS ON HEADS.
Meanwhile, without our knowledge, the conjectured
difficult child begins to understand
history. Do not refuse him his loss:
wanting things to change and to stay; briefly
comforted by snowfall.

49

Not to forget Colonel Fajuyi, dead
before I arrived (having lost out to Customs).
Thát means I was robbed; a sweat-pulped cache
of small ten-shilling notes (Nigerian). He
had wórse thíngs to contend with. I don't doubt
his courage, his slow dying – smell my fear! –
protracted hide and seek to the bushed kill. Faithful's
death was as foul but he ǀ went like Elijah.
Remaindered UN helmets, weapons, fatigues,
show up here, neo-tribal. Where did you
ditch the platoon? What have they done with Major
Nzeogwu's eyes?

52

Strange working of the body; how it knows
its ówn tíme. Thát after all ǀ and more –
seventy years near enough – the resin-knurled
damson tree, crookt at black gable-end,
stands in the sight of him departing. LÓRD ǀ
THOÚ HAST BEEN OUR DWELLING PLÁCE – FROM ÓNE
GENERÁTION ǀ TO ANÓTHER (lento). So barely
out of step ǀ bow and return. Charles Ives's
Ninetieth Psalm, found late, as grief's thánksgiving;
as full tide with ebb tide, the one in the other,

slow-settling bell arpeggios. Time, here renewed
ás tíme, hów it páces and salútes ús | in its wáys.

57

Shów you something. Shakespeare's elliptical
late syntax renders clear the occlusions,
cálls us to account. For what is abundance
understand redemption. Whó – where – are our
clowns | WET 'N' DRY: will the photographs
reveal all? Só hate to be caught in mid-
gesture, you knów thát, noble CARITAS,
proud AMOR – pledge your uncommon thoughts.
See all as miracle, a natural graft,
as mistletoe ravelling the winter boughs
with nests that shine. And some recensions
better than thát I should hope.

59

Everyone a self-trafficker. I asked
for stone and so received a toad. Alongside |
low-slung jets blizzard the surface-water,
jockey from gate to air-gate: next | the sea-gate
tilts out its lights. Blackness is to be
distinguished from blankness. The Laureates
process blank-faced for you to name them.
Did I sáy another trip ruined by bursts
of atrocious static, England My Country?
Mine, I say, *mine*: damn Skinflint's last onion.
And nów whose England áre you | but then whích
England wére you? Were you ever! NOW THEN!

64

In for the long haul. Course correction. Go
automatic until relief strikes you: spitted
up to – and beyond – the caecum. No sign there
of most-favoured malignancy. Meanwhile
the sitar's humming-bird finger-blur –
free in-house video, dizzying
play and replay: life's adjacent realm
with full and frank exchange of love-bites –
how coarse we are, I had forgotten. *Puir
auld sod*. Lift-off but no window. Leibniz's
monad is one thing. Óne thing or another –
we are altogether sómething else agaín.

65

Fragments of short score: inspirational I
find them. Visionary insights also
as they are called. Clouds of dark discernment
part wrath, part thankfulness, the full spectrum
rekindling; the rainbow still to be
fully wrought. Dón't say ˈ yoú have forgotten.
I HAVE FORGOTTEN MORE THAN YOU KNOW.
It is not nature but nurture ˈ brings
redemption to mind. *Mein Ariel,
hast du, der Luft nur ist . . .?* So name your own
sentence. Any sentence. You can have
life if you want it ˈ appeal to music.

71

I trust that she is now done with the body
search, close interrogation, the finger-
printing, the restless limbo of the *Quais*,
the depilatory and ritual bath,

the ultimate in cosmetics:
that, for the last time, she has wakened
to cameras, lust, vindictive protocol,
the snarl-ups in the lobby of false friends,
the go-betweens and other betrayers
to public knowledge. I cannot think how
else to commit, commend, her: a botched business,
out of our hands, reduced to the Sublime.

74

Bucer's England – *De Regno Christi* – even then
it was not on, not really. The more
you require it, the more it slips from focus,
skews in the frame, the true
commonweal out of true. Bucer knew this,
no-one exempted | nothing of fraudulent
greatness, even so. And Í say: accept
no substitute; but the body's natural
immunity to reason | you máy suffer;
at best by proxy. End of scholastic
disputation. Now the theatricals:
enter SCATOLOGY, *dancing, with* DESIRE.

77

Revive the antimasque of baroque
methane: time and death – thát rot, a fake
Shakespearean girning, a mouth's pained O,
the soul exhaled | as a perfect smoke-ring,
clownish efforts made to bind the corpse-jaw,
skeletal geezers like kids again with bad
joke-book toothache, Dr Donne's top-knot shroud,
coroneted bag-pudding (*show-off!*). Face
the all but final degradation – FAMED
PILLAR OF THE CHURCH A STIFF – reorder

the Jacobean Sermon, re-set Burton's
Anatomy, endorse the Resurrection.

79

Sleep as and when you can. Write this.
We are almost there. *Mein Ariel, hast du,*
der Luft nur ist . . .? Captive ˧ regain
immortality's incarnate lease. Endure
vigil's identity with entrapment.
There are worse obsessions. YOU HAVE MY LEAVE,
GO NOW ˧ free spirit shaped by captivity,
forsaken in the telling, so to speak,
the end of contemplation: overnight
the first frail ice ˧ edging across the pond,
self-making otherness by recognition –
even as I describe it.

80

Ice – *augenblick* – four chordal horns – baritone
invocation of mute powers. The grammar
of the centurion, formed to obedience,
pitched in disorder, unfocused zealotry. THIS
MÁY BE INSUBSTANTIAL. RESUBMIT.
The nadir of your triumph ˧ to do duty
in place of outright failure, erosions,
worn synapses. Even today the light
is beautiful – you can hardly avoid
seeing thát: shadows – reflections – on reeds
and grasses ˧ deepening visibility:
the mind's invisible cold conflagration.

81

Again: the saltmarsh in winter. By dawn
drain-mouths grow yellow beards. Old man's duty,
vigilance so engrained, shabby observance,
dirty habit, wavelets chinning the shore-line.
Rich in decrepit analogues ǀ he sees:
archipelagos, collops of sewage,
wormed ribs jutting through rime. Sun-glanced,
it is striking, vacant, a far consequence,
immaterial reflection beautifully
primed, the decommissioned lighthouse
no longer geared to darkness with clock-shifts
of steady alignment.

86

He voids each twelve-line blóck ǀ a head
solemnly breaking water. Not at thís time
Poseidon, but convulsively mortal,
spouting, eyes bulging, green man. Say again –
care to be psychic and by hów múch.
Is there ever a good time? What's on offer?
NIGHT AND FOG ǀ named as the losing answer
out of thousands submitted: albeit unjust
to slapdash courage. Not all is ruin
if you can hold a final salvo. Rouse
Hipper, advise floundering Jellicoe, make
signal of requiem, cast wreaths of iron.

88

Night and fog it ís then, comrades, *Nacht*
und Nebel: goes always for the throat –
pharynx, jugular. Ónce for áll cósts
of live demonstration waived. A few

dead women late admitted heroes
on generous terms. Sign here with broken
hands patched up for the occasion. Thank you
Odette, Violette, no further questions
commensurate with your knowledge. Stand at ease
against the wall. Unflattering photographs,
almost without exception, cracked and stained.
Darkest at finest hour. Add salt to taste.

89

Write out a cause: crazed sanity ‖ untreated
logomachic sarcoma. Unveiled stuff
of grand malpractice. Parts of the interlocked
post-doctrinal foul-up. Cheers! – Augustine's
fellow, who could fart – with most sweet savour –
angels' song: tones passing as angels' song.
Cross-reference ODOUR OF SANCTITY and run.
I give you ten yards cross-examination,
thwart man without allies (with friends, yes).
Don't overstretch it, asshole. Don't say TIME
WIPES ÁLL THINGS CLEAN. Don't let them hear CUR
DEUS HOMO – thát kind of filthy talk.

92

Either the thing moves, RAPMASTER, or it
does not. I disclaim spontaneity,
the appearance of which is power. I wíll
mátch you fake pindaric for trite
violence, evil twin. Here I address
fresh auditors: suppose you have gone the full
distance. Take up – ón líne – the true nature
of this achievement. Prove that you have fixed
the manifold. Dismiss the noń-appearance
of peculiar mercies. Presume to examine

the brain in its electric cauldron
regarding the Brazen Head.

93

Pardon is incumbent, RAPMASTER, ór it
is nót. On balance I thínk nót. So
get in line, SNÚFF-MAN — with PRINCE OF FEATHERS —
PRATFALL his oppo — mourning Persephone
lost in September tribute, England's daughter.
Hack violence to yourself ǀ brief miracle
confessions overridden. None of these
gífts us self-knowledge: she is beyond it
and you are nowhere ǀ spielers of abuse.
Slów búrn, slów double-táke. The Northampton
MADONNA AND CHILD. She there? Cán it be
the grief matronal? Í shall return to thát.

94

Hopefully, RAPMASTER, I can take stock
how best to oút-ráp you. Like Herod
raging in the street-pageants ǀ work the crowd.
Bít short of puff these days. Swíg any óne
elixir to revive the *membrum*. Squeeze
bóth tubes for instant bonding. IT'S HÍS CÁLL.
In the Algarve, places like that, the Brits
are heroes ǀ living as they háve to (*cheers*).
Where áre we? Lourdes? SOME sodding mystery tour.
Whát do you meán ǀ a break? Pisses me off.
Great singer Elton John though. CHRIST
ALMIGHTY — even the buses are kneeling!

96

Tune up an old saw: the name-broker
IS carnifex. Forms of enhanced
interrogation by the book. Footnotes
to explain BIRKENAU, BUCHENWALD, BURNHAM
BEECHES, DUMBARTON OAKS, HOLLYWOOD.
Masters of arts toiling as they are bent
to Saturn's justice in praetorian bunkers,
pourrying tortured figures from foundry sand
with suspect blood and their own fecal matter.
As many days as are the days of Sodom:
count áll one hundred and twenty | then shriek
I'M COMING.

98

TAKE TWO: the Northampton MADONNA AND CHILD:
an offering up of deep surfaces; chalk
sleepers from the underground | risen to this.
(Moore also became a figure.) Her bulk
and posture, load-bearing rt hip-bone,
inward, understood, projected, wrought.
The chíld's fáce, though, prím, sweetened, incúrious.
Absent here even the unfocused selving
close to vacuity – Stanley Spencer's fixation –
crazed-neighbourly | which ís a truth of England
alongside manifest others,
an energy altogether | of our kínd.

99

Hów many móre times? Customs not customs!
Fajuyi was dead by then, though Major Nzeogwu
still had his eyes. Can't you read English? What
do I meán by praise-songs? I could weep.

Thís is a praise-song. These are songs of praise.
Shall I hyphenate-fór-you? Syntax
is a dead language, your incoherence
the volatility of a dead age –
vintage Brook Farm, adulterate founders' bin;
and yoú the *faex Rómuli* | the dregs.
AUTHENTIC SELF a stinker; pass it on,
nasum in ano | the contagious circles.

102

A pale full sun, draining its winter light,
illuminates the bracken and the bracken-coloured
leaves of stubborn oak. Intermittently
the wínd spoórs | over sált ínlets
and the whiteish grass between the zones,
apprehension's covenant. Could this
perhaps end here: a *Paradiso*
not accounted for – unaccountable –
eternally in prospect, memory's blank
heliograph picketing the lost estate?
ÁND | ís this vision enough | unnamed, unknown
bird of immediate flight, of estuaries?

105

Absolutely untouched by the contingent –
ás he believes he ís – master
academician of rotor-wisdom,
indispensable, self-made, *thaumaturge*,
until dispensed with | disposed of. THÁT RÍGHT?
What is the present standing of injustice
among those who know? Would we – without Churchill –
have concluded a Vichy peace? That's
hard to say. Daventry and Droitwich
are still transmitting – cries of disbelief,

recognizance | evasions that return
with a comet's faithfulness of assignation.

106

DE MORTUIS – bitterness of those journeys:
the rail-ice thawed by acetylene
and coke braziers; chipped-free semaphore
arms tílting to right of way. *Arbeit,*
heraús, were nót words Í knew in those
deep years of the dead: the eight-coupled
coal engines, shaken viaducts, compounded
smoke of manufacture and destruction.
If you can still remember, put me down
as terror-stricken, unteachable.
Or hold me to my first promise. *Sadly*
I máy show up in time for yr lást laúgh.

110

ÁM discomfited | nót nów being able
to take as fact even my own dying –
the apprehension or prospect thereof. My
faux-legalisms | are to be vouched for,
even if unwitnessed, ás are many things
I could indicate but not show. Whát I see
here | are unfixable fell-gusts | ratching
the cranky chimney-cowls; their smókes blówn
hard dówn or túgged rágged; shade and shine
the chapel wind-vane's blistery fake gold.
I imagine | yoú see this also: súch
is the flare through memory of desire.

When all else fails CORINTHIANS will be read
by a man in too-tight shoes. No matter. You
shall not degrade or debauch the word LOVE
beyond redemption. As she redeems it.
Six times this trip I have brought round my wreath
to the vulgar gates. Let Thames take over,
not grandiosely, our plebeian grief.
Evangelical high prelates caught
spitting out plum stones [EDIT TAPE]. Guardsmen
make heroic bearers: even their wry-necks
crick in alignment. Comedienne to act
SORRY for hostile nation. CURTAINS. CREDITS.

115

Where CODA to the CITY OF GOD? Restore
whát decrepit organ? Whó has a mind
to improvise? You say it is áll
improvisation – dú, mein Ariel.
Shove off, there's a love. Under half-dead
wisteria, crudely cut back, the stone
lintel, newly snail-cobbled, glitters
with their mucilage. Not bad as an aubade;
not quite the final gasp. Extrapolate
LAST POST into reveille. Re evil –
relive, revile, revalue ǀ self-
revelation. EASY NOW, SOUL-BROTHER!

116

Hów could you have lived thróugh him ǀ so long?
Don't take it for an accusation – you
write as if sleep-walking. I never
walk in my sleep. I fall off chairs. But –

yes – it's a lengthy haul to the diploma.
Self-correction without tears: see me reverse
tango this juggernaut onto the road.
TEN DEGREES BACKWARD, Isaiah says.
Ezekiel's the better mechanic but less –
you know – beautiful! Áll eighteen
wheels engaging the hardtop and no
body-damage to speak of. RIDE IT, PREACHER!

118

Inconstant even in this the dead
heart of the matter: laughter | no joy.
Thin veil of libel úp for bids. You áre
wantonly obscure, *man sagt*. ACCESSIBLE
traded as DEMOCRATIC, he answers
as he answers móst things these days | easily.
Except in thís one craft he shows himself
open to a fault, shaken by others' weeping;
duty's memorialist | for the known-unknown
servants of Empire – for such unburied:
the spirit's gift upheld, impenetrable;
the bone-cage speared by lilies of the veldt.

119

Shambles of peripeteia to discover
history íf not to make it. Loud laughter
track | poór compensation for the bád shów.
This needs working on but then who needs it?
AMICUS, his own worst enemy? Make a good
ending, as they used to say. So gíve me
yoúr prescription for the good life and I
will teár throúgh it. Dissever sensual
from sensuous, licence from freedom; choose
between real status and real authority.

Clever móve thát – Catullus's sure-
foóted imitation | of the Límper.

English Limper | after the English Sapphic. Thís
hás to be seen. But whát a way to go.
Given a free mínd Í would present Daumier's
effigies as supreme honours: goúged,
wrenched, and sagging clay; self-made
corruption ravaged | inexhaustible,
FUROR'S own purity. *English*, you clówn –
líke at the ALDWYCH. So whát cognómen
will become me at last? O TIME-LIFE, dó
try to be reasonable; you háve the power.
At least pass me the oxygen. Too late.
AMOR. MAN IN A COMA, MA'AM. NEMO. AMEN.

The Orchards of Syon

I

Now there is no due season. Do not
mourn unduly. You have sometimes said
that I project a show more
stressful than delightful. Watch my hands
confabulate their shadowed rhetoric,
gestures of benediction; maledictions
by arrangement. For us there is
no deadline, neither for stand nor standoff.
I can prolong the act at times
to rival Augustine, this shutter
play among words, befitting
a pact with light, the contra-Faustian heist
from judgement to mercy.
I shall promote our going and coming,
as shadows, in expressive light; take
my belief, if only through a process
taxing salvation – may I proceed? –
not merely to divert with faith and fiction,
to ease peregrination, what a life!
Has it ever been staged
seriously outside Spain, I mean
La vida es sueño? Tell me, is this the way
to the Orchards of Syon
where I left you thinking I would return?

III

La vida es sueño as shadow-play. This
takes me back. Genuflect to the gutted
tabernacle, no-one will wonder in what sense
words are consequential to the cartoon.
How is this life adjudged
derelict, a stress-bearer since Eden?
Think ahead: your name
finally out of alignment, its
dates crammed in; they might be self-inflicted
wounds of morose delectation
borne lightly out of primal throes, a last
remittance from doomed childhood.
Unwise or wise choices do make
gymnasts of anchorites, if that
means what I mean. You say you have me there
which is all we have here, in the Orchards
of Syon that are like Goldengrove
season beyond season. Neither day nor hour
to determine the tinder
chemistry of exchange. If I were you, would
you believe? Ripe vastage of estate,
the Fall revived with death-songs. Set this down
as anomy's coherence, and the full-
blooded scrub maples torch themselves in the swamp.

IV

We are – what, all of us? – near death. So wave
me your solution. *Cupio dissolvi,*
Saul's vital near-death experience more
sandblasted than lasered. *Beam
us up, Asrael.* High talk, dissolution
expansive, all pervasive; here it coils
back into density: dark angel, fused,
rubberoid, shrunk, foetal, as though raked
from Zeppelin ashes. Immortal
Death, lovely suppliant!
Orphée I saw six times in the one week.
Du calme counsels the Princess, Maria
Casarès, newly *enceinte* with sorrow
not hers alone. Her tragic shadow – pulled
through – down and across – is swept
off the blank end wall. Truth not so hot,
unobliging, even at the last count.
I understand Hell's surreal ruins to be
those of the blitzed Académie de St Cyr,
with wind machines off camera, all elements
miming a solemn music.
Bite on yr death wish. As for faith,
expose it finally, like ignorance.
Coming or going, do the circuits again.

IX

The year rounds, takes fragments round with it. Some
tryst this is, image-conscious iconoclast!
The well-worn pattern, familiar abutments,
abraded angles, in the nature of limestone,
unfinished to perfection. Say something, you
have a name for it. Curlews on call,
high and abroad, to be identified
quartering the topmost fields; and other
alarm cries, known but not placed, *chich
chich, chich chich*. Penumbrate, a lily
distinctly shines, talisman
to that which is key-cold ín me, and sealed.
Could be haemony, from some remote
and gracious fable, upholding the rod
or stem of sharp judgement, finally spared.
Are you still with us, spirit of difficult
forgiveness íf I may so term you? The man
is old; it is more than age he girns for.
And Í said: is there anything you think
you should tell me? Was there a mirror
and did it breathe cold speculation?
He is knackered and there are no
schemes to revive him. The year unlocks,
hunkers, swings, its anniversary-round.

XI

Begin with golden curtains; sometimes helps
to anticipate THE END. How did they make
insouciant comedy so like innocence?
By way of Ealing, charm in confusion
through to last checkpoints. Impudent,
feckless. Watch them frogmarched off.
The Day of Judgement (WATTS) dire codicil
to human mood and thought; elect
doctrine on show, its common other side
exposed in saturnalia. I salute
yr good self – the stout party – bounding
egalitarian cockiness its *forte*,
sensual, unfallen. Dreams have charted
levels of sleep both complex and perplexing
I understand. It's a safe bet we're all
potentially impotent. Again, you coúld
say that I give myself
to well-failed causes. If this failed
to make the last connection I'd be sorry
from my own viewpoint, rarely now entranced
by calf love, light-fingered cockneys. Pimlico
is not Silvertown | though,
on the screen, it might appear so. Exit –
through heavy resistant side-doors – in a daze.

XII

Might gain eras of promise, collages
of dashed peace, many-headed the field
rose, dog rose, tossing in bright squalls,
all things self-verifying. A ferrous
atmospheric tang between lightning-bouts
has similar potencies, its presentiments
in the instant abundance, superflux,
familiar chill inspiration, self-
charged shock beyond shock. Show how many
succeed, rising again undiscovered,
turning at a breath: exhalation,
threshold and lintel, the unknown
to be entered, yet to be desired;
on a timekeeper's schedule if need be.
Exhalation, ah, not inspiration! the Orchards
of Syon exhaling green into gold,
gold to candescent red. Like ancient
rhetoric, both florid and threadbare,
showing the *stemma*. Light-endowed
among the natural shades and shadows; heavy-
browed barbed rugosa, rain-hackled, a streaming
instant unreconciled, magnificently
thrown off – the coda,
the invoked finality ‖ the setting-out.

XIII

No: blessing not mercy. Not that I care
to chance it. Unless there glints our ransom.
Centuries of failed initiates exclaim
against these equities. Whatever
your name is, leaden Mercurius.
Let me review a sometime common
standing or vantage. Patchy weather, quick
showers gusting the fields like clouds of lime.
You thought us held by favours: see above.
Such are the starts of memory, abrupt
blessing slid from confusion. Await
new-fangled light, the slate roofs briefly
caught in scale-nets of silver, then
sheened with thin oils. These signals
I take as apprehension, new-aligned
poetry with truth, and Syon's Orchards
uncannily of the earth.
JEFFERIES' *ancient sunlight*, Williamson
perhaps turning more profit by the phrase.
But pass me over, angel. I've recast
my furthest revelation; it's as much
as you have witnessed, much as I have told:
a massive, shedding, insubstantial substance
blurred and refocused, blurred afresh by rain.

XIV

The fell, through brimming heat-haze, ashen grey,
in a few hours changes to graphite, coral,
rare Libyan sand colour or banded spectrum.
Distant flocks merge into limestone's half-light.
The full moon, now, rears with unhastening speed,
sketches the black ridge-end, slides thin lustre
downward aslant its gouged and watered scree.
Awe is not peace, not one of the sacred
duties in mediation. Memory
finds substance in itself. Whatever's brought,
one to the other, masking and unmasking,
by each particular shift of clarity
wrought and obscurely broken-in upon,
of serene witness, neither mine nor yours,
I will ask bristling centaury to translate.
Saved by immersion, sleep, forgetfulness,
the tinctured willow and frail-textured ash,
untrodden fern-sheaves, a raw-horned oak,
the wavering argents in the darkened river.
Later again, far higher on the fell,
a solitary lamp, *notturna lampa*,
night's focus focusing, LEOPARDI saw,
himself a stranger, once, returning late,
from some forsaken village festival.

XVII

Tri-towers, Christ-silos, rise from, retract
into, the broad Ouse levels. Roadside poppies,
hedged bindweed, still beautiful. The kempt fields
basking; intense the murmur of full summer,
more growl than murmur: coast-traffic snarled,
snarling. Hawks over the dual carriageways.
I've jolted from northward across the moors,
not entirely at peace. Memoranda for horizons
in travail – spirit-levels – steadiness
of outlook all too readily measured.
Broadly, I have the measure of myself,
mechanically at bay. I'd not resurrect
Goldengrove, other than as a grove in Syon:
sustainable anomaly, so I
can tell you, though too easily said.
Tommies' lore, re crucifixes and the like;
Tennyson's wild expenditure of bells;
suffering – Gurney's – his queer
politics; Owen transfixed by eros:
my difficulties are not with their
forever-earnest speech. The chorus
lines of road-rage shunt to yet more delay.
Masked somewhere, on one side or the other,
the time-struck Minster doles greed by the clock.

XVIII

Comedic my control: with each new old
scenario, keep moving. In the Orchards
of Syon you can delve Los Angeles
or some other holy place.
Havergal Brian's Five Towns extorted
wealth from poverty, but with choral music
held as a birthright: well-tended ground
ripe for laying waste, the Great War.
Lawrence's Eastwood, Rosenberg
in Stepney and Whitechapel – I'm
ordered to speak plainly, let what ís
speak for itself, not to redeem the time
but to get even with it.
Glastonbury mislodged on its mud lake
with jackpot ignorance and freakish thorn;
York trafficking, gridlocking, organ-congas,
medieval hell-mouths less congested
than this sullen Minster. Anarchy coheres.
Incoherence coheres. Stupor animates.
Chaos ordains. But to what depth? Some demon
chobbles its rap-cassette, spits out
pathetic dreadlocks. I had forgotten
Donne's meta-theology. A road-drill
swallowed through tarred slab re-emerges fighting.

XX

Two nights' and three days' rain, with the Hodder
well up, over its alder roots; tumblings
of shaly late storm light; the despised
ragwort, luminous, standing out,
stereoscopically, across twenty yards,
on the farther bank. The congregants
of air and water, of swift reflection,
vanish between the brightness and shadow.
Mortal beauty is alienation; or not,
as I see it. The rest passagework,
settled beforehand, variable, to be lived through
as far as one can, with uncertain
tenure. Downstream from this Quaker outcrop
Stonyhurst's ample terraces confer
with the violent, comely
nature of Loyola and English weather;
stone, *pelouse*, untouched by carbon droppings,
now, from the spent mills. Indescribable,
a word accustomed through its halting
promptness, comes to be inscribed. The old
artifice so immediate, the delight
comprehends our measure: knowledge granted
at the final withholding, the image that is
to die, the creature, the rock of transience.

XXIII

Not all palimpsests are this eroded
to mý mind. A late sun buffs the granite.
Autumn lies lightly earthed, her funerals
the yellowed reddle blown bare, still abundant.
Should I say só much for Elijah's
chariot blessing these banked fires? If that
were even half-true I could give my name
to rehabilitation. *Bien-aimées*,
this calls for matching alchemies to make
gold out of loss in the dead season:
Petrarch revived by CHAR, though not
in so many words, *la flamme sous l'abri*,
the curfew-flame, uncovered. Frénaud,
bleakly resplendent. *Where are you fróm?*
I said; and he said, *Montceau –
Montceau-les-Mines.*
Once you ask that you can direct this,
objectify fear, sorrow; the well-placed
lip-readers of failure now succeed.
Last days, last things, loom on: I write
to astonish myself. So much for all
plain speaking. Enter
sign under *signum*, I should be so lucky,
false cadence but an ending. Not there yet.

XXIV

Too many times I wake on the wrong
side of the sudden doors, as cloud-
smoke sets the dawn moon into rough eclipse,
though why in the world this light is not
revealed, even so, the paths plum-coloured,
slippery with bruised leaves; shrouded the clear
ponds below Kenwood; such recollection
no more absent from the sorrow-tread
than I from your phantom showings, Goldengrove.
I dreamed I had wakened before this
and not recognized the place, its forever
arbitrary boundaries re-sited,
re-circuited. In no time at all
there's neither duration nor eternity.
Look! – crowning the little rise, that bush,
copper-gold, trembles like a bee swarm.
COLERIDGE's *living powers*, and other
sacrednesses, whose asylum this was,
did not ordain the sun; but still it serves,
bringing on strongly now each flame-recognizance,
hermeneutics of autumn, time's
continuities tearing us apart.
Make this do for a lifetime, I tell myself.
Rot we shall have for bearing either way.

XXVIII

Wintry swamp-thickets, brush-heaps of burnt light.
The sky cast-iron, livid with unshed snow.
I cannot say what it is that best
survives these desolations. Something does,
unlovely; indomitable as the mink.
Raise this with the sometime Overseer
for his stiff *Compliments Book*. Nothing left
to take leave of, if by any chance
you happened to be dying before colour
variety leapt to the blank screen. That
helps me to place my thoughts: intelligence
withdrawn convincingly from the eyes
awaiting close-down. Nothing prepares us
for such fidelity of observation,
I would observe. Nothing to be struck out
of like finalities. *Atemwende*,
CELAN almost at last gasp, *atem-
wende*, breath-hitch, say; or HARDY, *The Souls
of the Slain*. According to my
palimpsest, always the first despairing
calculation shows through. Frozen
irresolution, eternal stasis;
wintry swamp-thickets, brush-heaps of burnt light,
the sky cast-iron, livid with unshed snow.

XXX

Blurring sharpens: instance, my cold-tears make
flowerets, faceted clusters, out of clear brights,
headlights, eight, twelve, across, signal gantries
like emporium-glitter. I'm not driving
fortunately. How slowly it all goes
hurtling to oblivion. Line after line
solidly fractured *without*
effort and without discord – COLERIDGE; the eye
of Imagination passive and a seer.
Think seer as you would stayer. Even
thinking at all earns points; but if this
is the home-straight, where is my fixed home?
City of God unlikely. Then *in medias*
res, interactive with inertia? Or
something fazed mentors called the *lyric cry?*
You can cross frontiers in suspended
animation, homing onto the inner voice.
Lyric cry lyric cry lyric cry, I'll
give them lyric cry!
Whose is the voice, faint, injured and ghostly,
trapped in this cell phone, if it is not mine?
Some voices ride easily the current. Some
lives get away with murder any road.
How slowly – *without discord* – all hurls to oblivion.

XXXI

Yield violence to violence: no end yet
in pain's finale. Who was it said *Wood
of the Suicides?* I had imagined
that was behind us with *The Death of Virgil*:
the hemlocks' rugged outline, sleet-
welded, wind-harrowed, snow-haggard.
Not even halfway tired, I am fed
voices, *neque Hesperus, neque Lucifer,
sic admirabilis est*: Hesperus,
Lucifer, the strong planet that shines
as it sings, beautifully, in the clear
dome of midwinter. DANTE's trope
of Justice: my wounds your injuries,
why do these gird us so or edify
such undistinguished tears? *Atemwende:*
catch-breath, breath-ply. If you survive me,
do something with the incorrigible
nature of judgement. This is the way
a mind sits, congested and vacant,
sweating itself at a year's end:
breath-plight and remission, though I can mouse
no conclusion at this point, the live
screen blizzarded with interference – did I turn
myself on? – overriding MESSIAH.

XXXII

Black, broken-wattled, hedges appear
thinned through, fields an irregular patchwork,
the snow businesslike. I can record
these elements, this bleak satiety:
accustomed ratios of shine to shadow
reversed; inflected when not reversed.
Closer to nightfall the surface light is low-toned.
This is England; ah, love, you must *see* that;
her nature sensing its continuum
with the Beatific Vision. *Atemwende*,
breath-fetch, the eye no more deceived,
beggars translation. Her decencies
stand bare, not barely stand. In the skeletal
Orchards of Syon are flowers
long vanished; I will consult their names.
Climate, gravity, featherlight aesthetics,
pull us down. The extremities of life
draw together. This last embodiment
indefinitely loaned, not quite
the creator's dying gift regardless.
Clear sky, the snow bare-bright. Loud, peat-sodden,
the swaling Hodder. Of itself
age has no pull. Be easy. With immense
labour he can call it a day.

XXXVI

Downhill to go, then up the long curve of field.
December chastens the stream bed; frosted mist
hangs in autumn's leasowe; the far slope
burns hazy yellow where it is spring. I count
our seasons clockwise, with nadir and zenith,
on the year's face. Between five and six, that's
all I can see to tell you. The life-lines
tug briefly, my coming from way back, a child's
journey between worlds: though this is at best
half the fable. *Atemwende*, turn
of breath. *Spinnrad*, turn of wheel. Many
returns melt barriers and the winged
lion roars his obeisance. Not good
chiasma if you cannot make crossing.
Babylon's candles are lit for children
far older than their time, of whom fondly
no-one despairs. I did the Lady
Julian an injustice
which I will leave for evidence against me,
configured by the final stroke. Of course
Hell is empty; or *The End* will erase it
in its due place and order. *Poets
leap over death* – was that COLERIDGE? If so,
did anyone see him do it and live?

XXXIX

I must have written this off-stage, if it
shows. Be serious. I repeat: ageing
is weirder far than our dying. *Quod erat
demonstrandum*, the sun in the stair-well
x-rayed thin dresses. Sensualist
memory, here Í am in this frayed
cyclorama, caught squinting absurdly;
and there is the joker with two heads. Intense
unwasted life, so nearly at an end,
what can I say now, except *Whose wére you?*
Hand out the book prizes, my acceptance
speech is postponed. *Your Children's
Health Under Labour* by BRUCE L. OSIS
and T. B. D. KLINING. What gives? An old
artery slurried with carbide. Language
destroys ideas but not character,
Mercurius. So what díd the Surreal
say to you that now bears repeating
like the ancient power of *Perforce?* Read
Dante's jokes about sex, though best not
for comfort, or pity. Furiously the earth
turns, but without sensation, the moon
adjusts herself to our perspectives. If joy
ís still in waiting, then let it be called.

XLII

Up against ageing and dying I stand bemused
by labours of flight: a low-geared heron
retiring to its pool, the shapes that gulls
beat and tack; a motionless
crow butting a head-wind, like carved beam-end;
the smallest birds also that ricochet
from bush to bush but strike nothing; kestrel,
slammed against window-glass, spread-eagled there;
wrenched updraught; slighted harpies
of witness, finally. Lepidoptera
drugged by light into shell havens
of self-destruction. Should these not tally,
metal-toothed winter oak-leaves rap
on shuttered mansards; a trumpet pitches
its high reflection. Something also of grief
baffled, murmurings of Kaddish
proscribed during the Passover; a raw
coffin discreetly manhandled. Cindered gusts
make their eyes water. I record this
among the scattered thrown-out accusations
proper to such scenes; think further of ABE
KLEIN's Uncle Melech, coming in low across
land newly called Israel, and held to be
unforgiving, that shadow-path a pledged curse.

XLV

Listen, Meister Eckhart is here, ready
and eager to tell us his great news:
that we caught aright the revelatory
scream from the carrousel; that there's a divine
presence in destitution; that yes, we loved
bright Harry Heine and Frank O'Hara
as more than passing attractions when
I pass was the catch-phrase and they unheard of;
that the heavy residues from easy loving
render us breathless. Both you and I
who pray with the *dévots* yet practise
every trick in the book: our nuptials
are of the spirit entirely. The topos
of the whole is gratitude. Duino's
cliff-hanger we witnessed, and its consummation.
Wait, I've not finished. A radical
otherness, as it's called, answers
to its own voices: that there should be
language, rituals, weddings, and wedding-nights,
and tapes which spin fast forward, stop, reverse;
that there is even now hawthorn, this bush
pregnant with the wild scent and taint of sex;
that there áre men and women, destinies
interlocked; and dying, and resurrection.

XLVIII

But what a hope, but to have willed so much
upon you. As if I were my true self,
myself the other. Not that you claim this
but we have to invent dialogue – don't ask –
like patience provoked into being. Then
what should I say these are: the gates
of Emanation? Not if you can help?
Pub car-park puddles, radiant cauls of oil.
When all else fails, the great rainbow, as Bert
Lawrence saw it or summoned it. *Va' via!*
but not remotely. The entire display
swings on a fulcrum and is repositioned
as the earth tilts and spins. You need to weigh this
by constant reckoning. I am not the judge;
these are not directions. Never let
my voice mislead you. I may be mistaken;
self-mistaken; wrongly self-possessed;
confusing jealousy with righteousness
as I would have it
whatever wrongs we do, one to another;
our midlands far and wide; LAWRENCE, his
New Jerusalem *in the mind enthroned*,
time for bestowal, shadow into shadow,
St John the Baptist gloaming on its hill.

XLIX

In due consideration of the world's
bulk and selvage, I envision the Orchards
of Syon in terra cotta and yellow brick;
tracts of juniper; beauty still thriving
on squatters' rights. What was Lawrence's
view of *The Blind Girl* if he ever saw it –
he múst have – the two rainbows, the young
woman, unseeing herself, but taken
out of the body, as we are, blindly,
by self-forgetting? The sun, the sudden
prism, rediscover their own time,
whenever that is; bending to our level
they lift us up. Hopkins, who was self-
belaboured, crushed, cried out being uplifted, and he
was stronger than most. He said that creatures
praise the Creator, but are ignorant
of what they do. Imagine your own way
out of necessity; imagine
no need to do this. Good story, bad
ending, if narrative is the element
that so overreaches. Providence
used to be worked-in, somewhere. I, at best,
conjecture divination. The rainbow's
appearance covenants with reality.

LIV

Memory is its own vision, a gift of sight,
from which thought step aside, and frequently,
into the present, where we have possession
more and more denied us. I shall not
deny yoú without recollection.
Query: how far ascribe this to a failed,
no, failing, motor control. I am not less
careful or curious of our durance, *the eye's
elaboration of tears*, MRS BEETON'S
beautiful phrase. She failed at twenty-eight
and went unwept by me. Now you also,
sine nomine, if that is what you are,
earthy-etherial, I desire you
to fathom what I mean. What dó I mean?
I think you are a muse or something,
though too early rejected. The dank
Triassic marl, sandstone like mouldered plaster,
can't all-inhold you. From Burcot to Worms Ash
the rock sweats and trickles, even in winter,
the sun digs silver out of the evergreen.
Orchards of Syon, tenebrous thresholds
of illumination, a Latin love
elegist would comprehend your being
a feature of his everlasting dark.

LV

I desire so not to deny desire's
intransigence. To you I stand
answerable. Correction: must once have stood.
What's this thing, like a clown's eyebrow-brush?
O my lady, it is the fool's confession,
weeping greasepaint, all paint and rhetoric.
Empower the muse; I'm tired. Shakespeare, who scarcely
brooded on perfection, perfect so many times.
Memory! memory! *The eye
elaborates its tears*, but misremembered,
misremembering no less key-clustered
mistletoe, the orchard's châtelaine.
I may well carry my three engraved thoughts
out beyond Shrawley whose broad verges once
throve like spare garden plots with pear and apple
or with wild damson, thinner on the ground.
O my lady, this is a fool's profession
and you may be dead, or with Alzheimer's,
or happily still adoring a different
Duke of Illyria. I have set you up,
I confess thát, so as not to stint
your voice of justice. Love grows in some
way closer to withdrawn theology.
The Deists' orb drops below Ankerdine.

LVII

Reading Dante in a mood of angry dislike
for my fellow sufferers and for myself
that I dislike them. Dante is exact
in these conferrals. The words of justice
move on his abacus or make a sudden
psst psst like farrier's hot iron on horn.
The small blue flame of the glass votive lamp
that jibs in the funnelled air at the right
hand of Mary Mediatrix is his also.
From this distance the many barbed divisions
between Purgatory and Hell appear blurred.
You could step across or shake hands. Logic
is fierce, though at the last less feral
than mock-logic that destroys many.
Sensuous is not sensual, but such knowledge
increases with sensuality – *psst psst* –
hissing and crying out, the final throes.
Messaline – FRÉNAUD – *la vulve*
insomnieuse – ever-working valve-part
unsightly, blood-gravid. Look, Virgin
of Czestochowa, shelterer
from the black rain, look, ser Brunetto
whom Dante loved, look, Farinata: the sun
moves a notch forward on the great wheel.

LXV

Not quite heat- or rain-scrim, this heavy
blankness, thinning now, presides with a mauve-
tinted wipe-around grey. Noon, yet no distance
to any horizon. The Malverns gone in haze.
I would not, formerly,
have so described bereavement. *Land
of Unlikeness* a similitude, certitude
moves to dissolution. Still, an answer:
misprised, misplaced love,
our routine, is not tragedy;
misadventure at worst. And my self-styled
lament must cover for us both.
Something here to know time by, in all
conscience. In all conscience we
shall lie down together. Dear one, be told
you chose impenetrable absence; I became
commonplace fantasy's
life-sentenced ghost. Allow
our one tolerable *scena* its two minds.
Abruptly the sun's out, striking a new
cleave; skidding the ridge-grass, down steep hangers;
buddleia in dark bloom; a wayward covey
of cabbage-whites this instant I balanced
and prinking; the light itself aromatic.

LXVI

Belated grief-dervish: moribund and only
now into the surge and swing of the elements.
And not my words alone, as I commit them
to you also, yoú being my last but one
love. This could as well be lichened rock
or shadows of stained glass, Rossetti-like,
glowing and fading; ebbing, you might say.
Thát tell you what love is, how it stands, how
it opens itself, mirrors itself blind;
how it is self-requiring, not disarmed;
who makes it, who falls hard by the way
like carnal Christians or lost picaros;
poorly attended, guarded, self-exposed,
self-perpetuating, selfless, barren;
poison ivy or shingles for hair-shirt?
Imagination under stress in due
time becomes carbon, which I will not waste.
Who needs retractions? I can torment myself
with simple gratitude, municipal
salvias in the restyled garden of rest
staring my thoughts back. Beleaguered, roughly
unhostile people, many voices raised;
Messiah and *Elijah* filling the slate-
roofed tabernacles of millstone grit.

LXXII

Never an off season. Call for the voicer
of fair omen. The voice persists
in rising monotone. Talk obsession
to ecstasy. Switch off *My Word*. Lie
down in the space provided.
Pollen and basalt – Dame Rainbow, ancient
lover of water, immortal
for want of a better term; self-remnant
in each element of the same desire.
Not as she once was, metaphysical
and, like, wild. Weigh the importunate
nature of being | with a light
husk, the grasshopper's, tall
storyteller of the Hesperides
with hymns to divine Aphasia
(*for it is she*). Even so Goldengrove
might have been Silvertown, could be Golders Green;
you can't rule on that. *Finis* was the last
word to escape me. Period. Stop
trying to amuse with such gleeful sorrow.
Here are the Orchards of Syon, neither wisdom
nor illusion of wisdom, not
compensation, not recompense: the Orchards
of Syon whatever harvests we bring them.

Scenes from Comus

(1) The Argument of the Masque

I

Of the personality as a mask;
of character as self-founded, self-founding;
and of *the sacredness of the person*.

Of licence and exorbitance, of scheme
and fidelity; of custom and want of custom;
of dissimulation; of envy

and detraction. Of *bare preservation*,
of *obligation to mutual love*;
and of our covenants with language

contra tyrannos.

II

Sexual love – instinctively alchemical:
early sexual love. Or is the dying
recreation of it the real mystery?

I say that each is true: words troth-plight
to both of us, equal with her, truer
now, than I wás or ever could be,

but knowing myself in her. I said
ask me to explain – they won't remember,
forty-six lines back and already buried

with the short day.

12

That *marriage is a hieroglyphic*, stands
in its own garment. Not a possession.
Not always dispossessed. Or to speak

otherwise: it brings ruin and the numen
together; and indeed it cán
be a lovely thing when others make it so.

That numen, too, is a hieroglyph –
a shadow brought to bear, a signal.
And that reason is articulate in the will

if you don't think about it.

19

That from this noise, this mêlée, there issues
a grand and crabby music. And that I
want my piece of it. Even when not mine.

That vows so made are like lights on snow-ploughs,
purpose and power at once. Look what gets
tossed aside. Massive effects are junked.

And they talk about Heavy Metal! They don't know,
these kids, what weight of the word is,
that in the half dark of commodity most

offers are impositions.

(2) *Courtly Masquing Dances*
nello stile antico

18

This is a fabled England, vivid
in winter bareness; bleakly comforting,
the faded orchard's hover of grey-green.
We have come home, say, all is well between us.
Sharp-shining berries bleb a thorn, as blood
beads on a finger or a dove's breast pierced
by an invisible arrow to the heart.

22

Sharpened, sharpening, the swifts' wings
track and loop back clear skeins
through vanished arches.
See in what ways the river
lies padded – no, dashed – with light.
Show whether the imaged clouds
are litanies or escorts.

26

The corrupter, the abuser, the liverish
ravager of domestic peace. The soi-disant
harmless eccentric. Nobody's harmless.
Neither is comedy. Maybe the polka
injured thousands. In this depleted time
revive me, take me to a blue
movie, hold my hand in the dark.

37

Harrowed three days, now Lazarus
breaking his fast. Dead Sickert's look-alike.
Post-flu invalid's diet and inappropriate
light-squinnied isolation. Abstemious wolfing,
loose-tied, flop hung, baggy, nappy-cravat,
big dish of mussels, stewed prunes, gleaming black stones,
spoon like a tongue-depresser | gobbed straight in.
Poverty parodied – rich sensual man of parts –
death-grip on his revived inheritance.

44

I'm tired now the whole time and yet I wish to
take up my bed and walk:
to Compostela, for example,
bush-hat hung round with clamshells on return:
or ride the Gulf Stream through to Akureyri
and find a hot spring equal to my bulk
sheltered by palm trees, bowered by frangipani
or bougainvillia, wallowing in *Icelandic
Christian Poetry* till the fish come home.

46

The light – generous – discovers its ascent,
gives all it can bring us.
A haze, and at odd hours the moon also is there
appearing sea-worn.
But what a hope, the mild attrition
of a dove's call, the body
gradually winding down, becoming vacant.

79

No, no. Comus screamed like a peacock
at this conclusion. Moral vanity
is his parole, in the off season,
at any time mere sensuality
seems to lie dormant. I know well
the bristling strut, demonic rectitude,
the rod and glass, the masks of his fixation.

80

While the height-challenged sun fades, clouds become
as black-barren as lava, wholly motionless,
not an ashen wisp out of place, while the sun fades.
While the sun fades its fields glow with dark poppies.
Some plenary hand spreads out, to flaunt an end,
old gold imperial colours. Look back a shade –
Guþriþur Þorbjarnardottir – over your
left shoulder or mine ᛁ absolute night comes
high-stalking after us.

(3) A Description of the Antimasque

19

Nothing is unforgettable but guilt.
Guilt of the moment to be made eternal.
Reading immortal literature's a curse.

Beatrice in *The Changeling* makes me sweat
even more than Faustus' Helen, let alone
Marlowe's off-stage blasphemous fun with words

or Pound's last words to silence. Well,
let well alone. The gadgetry of nice
determinism mákes, breáks, comedians.

All the better if you go mad like Pound
(*grillo*, a grasshopper; *grido*, a cry from the fields).
The grief of comedy ǀ you have to laugh.

20

In Wintry solstice like the shorten'd light
sky closes; and sea parts, ranging itself
from unpredicted sources, radiant

when you'd guess blankness under broad shadow.
Hidden artificers ǀ of the visible
withhold what's long been destined to the dark.

In shifting scapes eternity resumes.
I cannot fault its nature, act by act,
gauged by the lost occasions of the sun.

Ephemera's durance, vast particulars
and still momentum measures of the void.
What did you say?

Without Title

Epiphany at Saint Mary and All Saints

The wise men, vulnerable in ageing plaster,
are borne as gifts
to be set down among the other treasures
in their familial strangeness, mystery's toys.

Below the church the Stour slovens
through its narrow cut.
On service roads the lights cast amber salt
slatted with a thin rain doubling as snow.

Showings are not unknown: a six-winged seraph
somewhere impends – it is the geste of invention,
not the creative but the creator spirit.
The night air sings a colder spell to come.

In Ipsley Church Lane (1)

More than ever I see through painters' eyes.
The white hedge-parsleys pall, the soot is on them.
Clogged thorn-blossom sticks, like burnt cauliflower,
to the festered hedge-rim. More than I care to think
I am *as one* coarsened by feckless grief.
Storm cloud and sun together bring out the yellow of stone.

But that's lyricism, as Father Guardini
equably names it: autosuggestion, mania,
working off a chagrin close to despair,
ridden by jealousy of all self-healed
in sexual love, each selving each, the gift
of that necessity their elect choice.

Later, as in late autumn, there will be
the mass-produced wax berries, and perhaps
an unearthed wasps' nest like a paper skull,
where fragile cauls of cobweb start to shine.
Where the quick spider mummifies its dead
rage shall move somnolent yet unappeased.

In Ipsley Church Lane (2)

Sage-green through olive to oxidised copper,
the rainward stone tower-face. Graveyard
blossom comes off in handfuls; the lilac
turned overnight a rough tobacco brown.
Every few minutes the drizzle shakes
itself like a dog:

substantially the world as is, its heavy body
and its lightnesses emblems, a glitter
held in keel-shaped dock leaves, varieties
of sameness, the pebbles I see sing
polychrome under rainwash,
arrayed in disarray, immortal raiment:

my question, since I am paid a retainer,
is whether the appearances, the astonishments,
stand in their own keepings finally
or are annulled through the changed measures of light.
Imagination, freakish, dashing every way,
defers annulment.

In Ipsley Church Lane (3)

One solstice has swung past, the immeasurably
varied, unvarying, profusion of hedge-burgeon
stays richly dulled, immoveable for a while.
Over by Studley the close air is dove-grey,
a hollow without sun
though heat had filled it; shadow-reservoir,

more than a mirage, however you chance to look,
if mirage-like in its reality.
The day does not wear well, the well-kept grounds
of the new offices are uninviting.
There is a kind of sullenness that summer
alone possesses. It passes; will have passed:

not to speak of your heart, that rules and lies
in webs of heavy blood, a clobbering fetish.
Parables come to order; the hurt
is mortal though endurances remain,
as they have to, insufferably so;
hindsight and foresight stationed in their ways.